BUILDING CALL CENTER
CULTURE

*Strategies for designing a
world class performance-based
environment within your
customer contact center*

DAN COEN

Design by Foglia Publications
408-970-9562
Edited by Marie Burkenheim

ISBN 0- 9660436 - 2- 6

A NOTE ABOUT TERMINOLOGY

Many terms and phrases in this book are used interchangeably, although they represent the same concepts. **_Call Center_** and **_Customer Contact Center_** are meant to have the same meaning in this book. Both phrases represent a place of work that involves the telephone, internet, web based chat, e-mail, customer and prospect relationships, and culture.

The term to describe personnel that communicate with prospects and clients via the telephone, web and e-mail are referred to in this book as **_Agents_**. Although your **_"Agents"_** may be called *representatives, telesales consultants, CSR's, inside sales representatives, client managers*, etc., one universal term, **_Agents_**, will be used to describe this function of employee.

The term **_Manager_** and **_Supervisor_** are used interchangeably. Both **_Manager_** and **_Supervisor_** are meant to represent those *coaches, team leaders, assistant coaches, department motivators and management personnel* holding any position that may have daily interaction and responsibility for call center operations, performance and culture.

ACKNOWLEDGEMENTS
AND DEDICATIONS

To those I have worked with — every person in every call center.
To my friends and family who provide me
with the motivation to succeed.
Together, you make interacting with
people an enjoyable treat!

CONTENTS

BUILDING CALL CENTER
CULTURE

Strategies for designing a world class performance-based environment within your customer contact center

DAN COEN

DCD Publishing

INTRODUCTION

I have written this book as a compendium for call center management because I feel there is a great lack of understanding from managers, supervisors and administrative staff about how to manage and inspire agents. Shaping call center performance is a tricky proposition. I have seen call center management painfully flail away at trying to motivate the very people who are critical to their success. I have been involved in meetings where the absolute arrogance and naivete of upper executives have sent call centers toppling to their knees, for little or no reason. I have seen upper management motivate supervisors through ignorant intimidation based on ill-conceived opinion. In turn, supervisors promote much the same attitude to their staff of agents. The culture of the call center becomes a world of disgust and mistrust. Agents feel like jailed squirrels with little outlets to communicate and less opportunity to advance. It is a vicious cycle. Have you ever been part of a call center where agents feel that management runs the operation like a jail? "Don't go to the restroom", "Why aren't you in your seat", "You aren't talking enough." Phrases like this make me wonder what a cell block must feel like. In many instances, agents can't walk in three minutes late without getting the evil glare. Supervisors can't sit down and think about what they want to accomplish in their day before upper management stampedes to their offices on an adrenaline-filled mission. This cycle is one that breeds failure. It promotes lost revenue. It allows competition that does its job just a little bit better to recruit your employees and gain an edge over your company.

This book studies the human science that impels call centers to rise and fall. It explores the intricate angles of communication and motivation that make call centers tick.

Through my management of call centers, I have tried and tested every piece of information in this book over and over again. I have succeeded, and failed, in a zillion different areas. More telling, I have failed to heed my own advice in more instances than I can count. In spite of all this, I have found dramatic _**successes**_ more often than failures. _**Success**_ in terms of the bottom line. _**Success**_ in terms of creating a strategic telesales and customer contact operation. _**Success**_ in terms of building agent performance. _**Success**_ in terms of shaping world class cultures that bring winning strategies to managers and agents on the front lines.

If you are a manager who supervises call center agents, then this book will provide you with detailed, strategic and creative ideas to ensure that your call center will <u>break both short term and long term records</u>. These ideas are not theoretical concepts. The strategies and philosophies presented here about call center management, the principles of the call center world and motivating and supervising call center agents are true, tried and tested in real-life customer contact centers. Each program—every idea and all tactics—have been used in the call center world over and over again to the benefit and success of thousands of people. This book explores the principles that motivate call center agents to perform at unparalleled success rates in the call center atmosphere. It challenges supervisors and managers to think differently from the way they presently do about how to get the most out of their call center agents and encourages management to create ideas and implement programs along those lines.

Each chapter studies the call center world from the perspective that people make up its victories and its defeats. We recognize that technology plays an enormous role in call centers today, and we incorporate strategies to combine the phenomenal advances in technology with the people who use those technologies. But it must be recognized that it is people who execute and propel performance. This book studies the human science that impels call centers to rise and fall. It explores the intricate angles of communication and motivation that make call centers tick.

Now that you know what you will find in this book, let's note what you will not find. Some books will provide charts and graphs on how to set up call center departments, create budgets to meet the bottom line, and sell over the telephone. Other books will dwell on statistical objectives, standard industry guidelines and service level approaches. This book spends very little time on those topics. Instead, this book exclusively explores the trenches of *people-to-people supervision* between management and agent.

One of the telling concepts you will find as you read and study this book encompasses the word "feedback". I noticed as I wrote chapter and page that I used the word "feedback" in so many areas that the word and its meanings became the primary influence to this entire book. Then, I began to recognize how often I utilize the theories of "feedback" in actual practice. When consulting with corporations and service agencies, or when presenting workshops, and even in casual focus groups, much of my discussions have focused upon utilizing "feedback" successfully. The importance of agent feedback cannot be understated, nor can feedback from management to agents, and among management and their peer groups. For instance, just consider the tremendous variables of feedback. Obviously, management requires employee feedback and vice versa. Certainly, feedback from outside customer to employee, and vice versa, is also necessary. Then, there are sub- variables to feedback. Positive feedback, negative feedback, proactive feedback, valuable feedback, irrelevant feedback, repetitive feedback, dynamite feedback, poor feedback, written feedback, verbal feedback, misunderstood feedback, well-meant feedback, vicious feedback, selfish feedback, overwhelming feedback, etc. Feedback shapes culture and culture breeds performance. When management masters the techniques of creating and implementing world class feedback, management will have the means to develop a form of communication that will drive all kinds of call center success. People, and businesses, thrive when they learn how to utilize feedback. It's that simple.

Building on that feedback note, I encourage feedback from you. I would relish the opportunity to speak with you on any topic. Most notably, I would like to hear your thoughts concerning this book, its theories of call center management, and any feedback you may have about ideas that you have instituted within your call center. All comments and suggestions are welcomed, as together we explore the phenomenal opportunities and creative possibilities that exist in call center management and operations.

Dan Coen
888-835-5326
818-703-1022
dcddcd@aol.com
www.dcdpublishing.com

CHAPTER 2

Six Fundamental Principles Of Call Center Management

"I can't figure out if call center supervision is an art or a science. I guess it is both."

Dan Coen

The Call Center Embodies Several Channels Of Communication

The call center is a world of communication. There are several channels that allow agent-to-supervisor and supervisor-to-agent communication to take place. When mastered successfully, a communication culture emerges that increases performance, attitude and retention across the board.

The Call Center Is An Emotional Environment

Agents and supervisors become emotional at the most inopportune times. Agents are not required to recognize, or handle, their emotions; supervisors are. The way supervisors manage their own emotions, and their agents' emotions, will dictate the level of success a call center exhibits. When supervisors fail to heed emotional challenges in the call center, supervisors lose their ability to effectively manage their employees.

Call Center Agents Are Motivated Based On The Feedback They Receive And The Feedback Systems That Supervisors Put In Place

During their professional careers, agents and supervisors have received zillions of pieces of feedback. How this feedback has impacted each agent or supervisor becomes evident in the practical work environment, where actions and thought processes are implemented based on prior feedback. Therefore, the conditioning that agents and supervisors experienced prior to their entrance in the call center sets the foundation for the call center environment.

Agent Performance Is Inconsistent When Management Is Inconsistent

Supervisors should see agents as mimics of their own performance patterns. This is because agents mimic their supervisors. The concepts, ideas, opinions and actions agents take are based on the conditioning they have received from their supervisors. Consistent patterns lend to comfortable agents who come up with consistent results.

The Call Center Must Employ Management That Is Able To Recognize How To Contribute Winning Ideas To Changing Dynamics

Creating opportunities by thinking differently is one step in the right direction. Channeling a supervisor's energy in order to implement creative thoughts and ideas is another step in the right direction. Lack of opportunity leads to stagnation. Stagnation ruins creativity.

There Is No Simple Classification Of Call Center Agents

There are new agents, senior agents, exhausted agents, exceptional agents, fledgling agents, involved agents, detached agents, comfortable agents, career-minded agents, aggressive agents, stagnant agents, entrepunurial agents, and motivated agents. Each agent falls into at least one category — many fall into more than one. Call Center performance increases when management supervises its employees using various classifications.

Agents are conditioned to perform. Their concepts, ideas and actions are based on professional and personal conditioning. Agents are conditioned to be consistent.

CHAPTER 3

Five Styles And Techniques Of Greeting Agents When They Walk Through The Door

"The best boss I ever had came into my office at the start of every day and gave me a rousing welcome. He knew that if I felt good about what I was doing, my agents would feel good about what they were doing."

Dan Coen

The call center game begins when the supervisor starts the process correctly. When supervisors fail to start the process correctly, agents fail to respond. The first thirty minutes of any call center shift should be controlled entirely by the supervisor, not the agents.

Do you feel that your call center lacks an introductory game plan each day? If you or your supervisors don't have a solid plan to keep your agents motivated and focused, then you are probably failing to do all you can do to affect performance, and retention. For instance, I once worked with a call center where two hundred and fifty agents began their day at 6:30am. At 6:30am, I would walk the call center floor and see four supervisors in one office, two supervisors in the break room, forty-five agents on the telephone, seventy-eight agents late or not at work, one hundred agents in the break room and rest rooms, and two supervisors on the floor working hard. In essence, supervision didn't start the call center game properly, and their agents followed suit. It was very disorienting. Imagine a restaurant where you seat yourself but no waiters come by to serve you, or a restaurant where you try to serve yourself at the buffet table but there is no food to be had. Imagine an airplane full of passengers while the pilots are in the employee lounge, or a stadium packed with fans while security and employees are late for work and just beginning to organize their duties.

It really doesn't matter how large your call center is. You may employ seven agents or seven hundred. The communication presented to call center agents in the first thirty minutes of their day will set the stage for the rest of the day. The best boss I ever had came into my office at the start of every day and gave me a rousing welcome. He knew that if I felt good about what I was doing, my agents would feel good about what they were doing. And he recognized that if he got me off to a rousing start, I would project that enthusiasm to my agents so they could get off to a rousing start, too. When that boss failed to come into my office every day to keep me motivated, I began to stop motivating my own employees. He fell into bad habits, and so did I. In turn, so did my agents. The first thirty minutes of any day is critical. Here are five ways to make those first thirty minutes work for you:

1. Condition your agents to expect something when they walk through the door

If all your agents walk through the door and scatter, thereby affecting the time they start on the telephones, here is the answer. Let your agents know that every morning you will present a message in one part of your call center. Perhaps it is in the back or front of the room, in the far corner, or in the breakroom. Placement is your choice. Utilize an overhead projector or white board, or multiple projectors and whiteboards, depending on the size of your call center. Each morning, have your supervisors guide the agents to that main spot in that certain part of the room. Your objective is to display a valuable message that your employees either *want* to read every morning, or *need* to read every morning. By doing so, you condition your agents to gather at the beginning of their shift, at one location. Then your supervisors can guide them to their desks so they may start work. Topics for your message could include yesterday's production, today's goals, congratulations for select high performers, service level results, contest announcements, company messages or contest winners. In time, you will find that more and more agents will rush every morning to the same location, merely to see something they believe has value. Management now has control over their agents. Management can now control what their agents do next.

2. Train agents to accept your objectives

Your agents will believe everything you say when they see that what you say matters, and is valuable. Therefore, when you forget to put up a message one day, you set a precedent that will endanger other decisions. When you fail to present an important message, or one of some value each day, you tell the agents your exercise is meaningless. But when you present a message every day and you put up valuable messages that inform, anything you do from then on will be looked at more closely.

3. Consistently penalize agents who fail to meet initial company objectives

I once worked at a boiler room that made me control agents this way: when the clock struck 7:15am, the doors were closed and locked. If the agent wasn't in the door at 7:15am, the agent went home. If it was Friday, the agent went to a dark room for 30 minutes where a supervisor came to get him and brought him back down to work, so all his peers could gawk at the latecomer. I hated that job, got a sore pain in my arm every day I went to work, and found better employment. What draconian measures!

But, in some ways, quite prescient. Agents were consistently penalized for failing to meet objectives. This policy stayed in effect for months. New hires felt it was a standard and historic policy and they followed it religiously. Old-timers adapted quickly for fear of not earning an income. Management was repulsed and I thought it was the wrong thing to do. But I learned from it, and so can you.

4. Make it a point of communicating with each agent in the same way each time

No matter how large a call center you supervise, you still may communicate with each agent every day. <u>Agents desire to have an opportunity to communicate with management in non-telephone communication.</u> Agents need to see and communicate with management in settings that don't involve penalty. Some ways of communicating with each agent each day are as follows:

1. Go to each agent, say "hello" and ask them how they are doing
2. Send a voice mail to each agent
3. Send an e-mail to each agent
4. Leave a message on the chair of each employee
5. Leave a personalized note on the desk of each employee

A little communication when it is not required is always welcome. What you go out of your way to do in three to thirty minutes' time pays dividends in every way imaginable.

5. Be prepared to motivate early. It pays dividends

I was always motivated by my boss only when I was ready to leave the company. It never worked. I left. He motivated late. I always motivated my agents when they were pleased with the company. It always worked. My agents stayed and excelled. I would leave. My agents would stay. My agents would then lose motivation. They would leave. If I were lucky, they would follow me. Then I had a core team wherever I went, and our teamwork and enthusiasm would rub off on everybody else. I motivated constantly, and I motivated my agents simplistically. I knew right from the beginning that if they recognized I had a vested interest in them, we would have a partnership and not a dictatorship.

CHAPTER 4

Designing A Spectacular Communication Culture

"Management must make the commitment to perform above and beyond the norms of creativity."
Dan Coen

The foundation of any call center operation begins and ends with the establishment and execution of a first-rate communication culture. A world class, phenomenal communication culture will bring your call center the best of success. I am not talking about the call center as a whole from Accounting to Xeroxing. I am talking specifically about the main floor; the place or places where your agents conduct their daily work. In that respect, Communication Culture embodies every aspect of the working environment between management, agents and the call center. Agents see the culture of their corporation through the communication culture of their department and supervisor, not through the corporate center. The reasons why call centers falter are not because the agents are not motivated, or because the supervisors are green, or because the compensation plan isn't proper. Those are the many effects from a particular cause. That cause is a fundamental lack of communication culture within the call center. Management should understand that a call center is a unique beast. A call center's whole basis of functioning properly revolves upon creating culture and building communication where agents and their telephones meet. My experiences have shown that senior executives may freely walk around their call center and easily identify areas of weakness when it comes to their existing culture. For instance, they may recognize that supervisors are not motivating the staff appropriately, or that agents may not be contributing successfully in their time away from the telephone. Where executives falter is when they attempt to solve *the problems they visualize*, instead of identifying and attacking *the root problems that are rocking the structure*.

> Poor supervisors don't understand the value of creating feedback opportunities. They recognize that communication is valuable, but they don't recognize how to present opportunities to their employees.

The lack of a strategic communication culture in the call center is the root problem. It involves every aspect of management and agent performance. Imagine communication culture as an overriding tenet of philosophies and practices that forms the foundation for everything that happens in the call center. It encompasses the structure of managing agents and supervisors on a daily basis; it encapsulates sales and customer service performance; it builds opportunities for feedback and growth; it overcomes roadblocks which invariably arise on an hourly, daily, and weekly basis. All that operates in the call center begins and functions through communication culture. There is no question that every call center, by nature, has some form of communication culture. Most probably, it is not the culture management wants. Or it may be the culture they want but not the culture they need. Management at all levels must recognize that a communication culture of some type exists in the call center today. The objective is to turn that communication culture into a world class dynamic.

Most call center managers understand the concepts of what they must accomplish. They recognize the reasons why agents don't perform to standards. They are able to articulate the theories as to what must be done to create opportunities. Yet, due to dozens of factors, those same managers don't have the time, energy or ability to take these concepts and bring them to fruition. They know the concepts. They have no ability to execute the actions.

Call center management is principally a compilation of theories and practicality. Whether you supervise five agents or 205 agents, the ebb and flow of daily operations involves a little bit of theory and quite a bit of implementation. I think of call center management in terms of 25/75. Twenty-five percent of a world class supervisor's job is based on understanding the philosophies and theoretical foundation of management. This 25% involves spending time away from the main floor thinking about the job, and about ways to increase performance levels. 75% of the job is doing; rolling up the sleeves and taking action by managing the agents who work the front lines. A call center supervisor can become quite polished at being great at the 25% of the job. But the supervisor will win or lose based on his ability to perform the 75% of his job at a spectacular pace.

Communication Culture begins by establishing dynamite communication for all employees, under the umbrella of a terrific culture for all employees. Those philosophies are not independent of one another. For instance, call center performance increases dramatically when management chooses to create an environment that recognizes all facets of communication. Communication that works in a call center starts with senior executives in chilly boardrooms and filters down to middle management in cramped offices. From this communication, front line supervisors and the very agents who will thrive and excel based on communication are conditioned to act. Exceptional communication includes such basics as consistent meetings, encouraged participation, follow-up and action plans from those meetings, the urging of agent feedback, channels of communication that provide energy and motivation to the call center floor, clearly outlined operating principles, open-door policies for all levels of management, succinct goals and objectives, etc. If one can imagine free and open communication, one can imagine the value of communication within the call center.

My experience in the call center has led me to believe that *asking questions* begins the process of forming outstanding communication culture. Asking questions is the key to building communication, and relationships, in the call center. I have spent thousands of days walking down one aisle of the call center and up the next aisle, stopping at each cubicle merely to ask questions of my employees. "How are you today? What is new in your world? How did you do yesterday? Whatever happened to the XYZ issue? Is there anything I can do to help you today? Is there anything you need from me? Are you having a good day?" These questions, while extremely basic, form the basis of a relationship. They build environment. These questions demonstrate to agents that management believes in more than a "do what I say" approach to call center supervision. Even when agents don't have any feedback to provide, the asking of questions begins the process of simple discovery. Asking questions, and discovering information about another person, is a strong principle which only the best supervisors recognize. People want to feel as if they are valued, and they want to believe that their supervisor values them in a way that their supervisor doesn't value other people. Showing interest in agents by asking questions to discover information about them sends that message.

A Call Center's basis revolves upon creating culture and building communication.

An example of asking questions and building communication culture can be seen in my special relationship with an agent I supervised for nearly three years. He was very extroverted when he had an issue, so as his supervisor I knew he was not shy about coming to me when he had an issue. Yet he stayed out of management's way when he had no issues; he stayed at his seat. Therefore, in order to communicate to him in a way that builds communication culture, I would come to his desk each morning two hours after the shift began and say "How's the day going?" His response, consistently, was "Terrible." My comeback regularly was "Good, good to hear it." The purpose of my question was to build culture — certainly, I wanted to know how his day was going, but that wasn't the objective of the question, and he knew this. I wanted to condition him to understand that two hours into the shift I would come by to check on him. The value of my coming by to check on him carried much more weight than the value of simply asking a basic question. The conditioning we developed allowed me to recognize how his day was *really* going. When he was having a great day, his tone and inflection would be quite different than when his day was truly awful. The goal in building communication culture with this agent, through question and discovery, was for me to show up on time each day and spend seven seconds inquiring how he was doing by using a simple question to evoke a simple response. This basic level of fun communication occurred nearly every day for three years. He became comfortable with my management style, and prospered in the environment.

Example of Poor Communication Culture:

Every time the vice president of the department is ready to make a policy change, he sends a memo to all management—out of the blue. No discussion, no interpersonal communications. This change might involve issues as serious as compensation adjustments, or as minor as a dress code announcement regarding Fridays. Such a memo, demanding action immediately, reflects the vice president's expectations that his management and agents are mere order-takers and robots.

Overcoming poor communication cannot be effectuated, however, unless a unique, creative and driven culture is formed to support the shift from poor communication to world-class communication. A culture must breed opportunity for all personnel. A culture must encourage and promote the chance to communicate. It must offer specific value-added benefits and opportunities to communicate. Communication Culture means creating an environment that allows agents and management to comment, create, propose, author, implement, strategize, improve or question, in some fashion, with the knowledge that their doing so counts. Communication can be created. Yet culture must be bred. In a nutshell, communication culture breathes life into its employees, its operations and its results.

I can recall using notes to stimulate positive communication culture with one very sweet and empathetic agent. When I would walk around the call center, she was very shy and always on the telephone. I couldn't pry her away from a call to ask her questions and create discovery opportunities. So, I used written notes to our advantage. First, I would leave her notes on her chair when she was at lunch or break, and she would write notes to me. I would then pick up the notes from her chair when she was away from her desk. Sometimes the notes were patterned in a simple paragraph format.

Other times, I used check marks and boxes to have her fill out multiple choice answers. The best part of this communication was that she had a chance, without me present, to comment, create, propose, author, implement, strategize, improve and question. There was no pressure to look me in the eye or think on her feet or answer questions on the spot, because I wasn't there. She had a chance to write down her thoughts and answers at her own pace. As I said just a paragraph before, a culture must encourage and promote the chance to communicate. Leaving notes and sharing letters gives agent and supervisor the chance to do so.

If you want your call center to build on the basic principles of communication culture, you might use the eleven topics below as a guide in that development:

1. Communication Culture encourages interactions among all parties in the call center.
2. Communication Culture balances concepts with execution.
3. Communication Culture builds a foundation to manage difficulties and challenges.
4. Communication Culture motivates all levels of employees to participate and transact in every facet of operations.
5. Communication Culture creates and sustains a cheerful and creative atmosphere for all levels of employees.
6. Communication Culture builds retention by ensuring the call center is a place employees *want* to be.
7. Communication Culture promotes residual training, cross-training, multi-dimensional jobs, and career growth.
8. Communication Culture incorporates a set of values, not a train of words.
9. Communication Culture establishes the structure that impacts performance.
10. Communication Culture continually revisits its goals, and is not afraid to reinvent itself.
11. Communication Culture employs a management staff that "gets it".

Please be cognizant that every call center has some element of a communication culture. It may resemble a prison, a bank, a basketball arena, Disneyland. Today, when you walk on your floor, your various senses can recognize your communication culture. Your senses can be trained to be as attued to communication culture as they are to food, body language, music, sights. The important thing to remember is that every call center does embody communication culture. Most call centers do not embody a world-class communication culture. Our job is to explain why.

Foremost, the challenges of creating a world class communication culture are daunting. Many management personnel believe their time, and their call center operational issues, are too important to invest in changing or creating from scratch a fantastic communication culture. Many executives have the opinion "if we're making money and things are sailing along, don't fix anything." With this philosophy, one can only imagine the type of culture that exists in the call center (Yuck). In addition, the great challenge in building a top communication culture is that it embodies everything to do with *people*. The eleven principles I mentioned above evoke human emotions, human thoughts, human conflicts, human feelings. They present opportunities and team challenges that management and staff may simply not be qualified to initiate. Consequently, even if executives want to implement a new and powerful communication culture, they may have difficulty finding the resources to gain buy-in from management and staff.

> **Communication Culture involves creating an environment which allows agents to participate. A communication culture can't be created from the top down. It needs to involve all levels of employees.**

In addition, any concepts regarding ways to make communication culture happen may be digested and manipulated differently by different people. Building consensus is tricky. If five parties want to try something nine different ways, how can accord be reached? In essence, why create a new communication culture for agents? The job of an agent is to work the telephone. Perhaps creating opportunities for one agent is a doable process. But creating opportunities for multiple agents is a bear. Why create a daunting task for supervisors and managers that may end up failing anyhow? Plus, challenges exist when it comes to buy-in. Creating a communication culture is a two-way street. Each of the eleven principles we mentioned above invites agents to contribute to building a communication culture. The process simply will not work without agent participation. Asking one or two agents to take initiative outside their daily telephone job is a doable process. But asking multiple agents to do so opens up issues. It's a well-known fact that when anything involves the interaction of many people, challenges abound, just as one-on-one basketball is easier to play than five-on-five, and small crowds are easier to manipulate than large crowds. It is no surprise then that agents wonder why they should invest their time and energy for a call center. Making agreements, carrying out duties and developing correct courses of actions can paralyze call centers and render any attempt to build communication culture moot if the participants don't agree to bind together. Introducing the objective of creating a new communication culture forces all staff to think about binding together. Management immediately takes a step back and says "Will our call center be able to make that leap?"

Even without knowing your call center, or assessing its operations structure, I can tell you the simple reason why management at all levels should embrace the notion of building a new communication culture. Management must view the call center as more than just a place to do business. In our society, many corporations see their business as a place employees should come to and go from, with the simple goal of doing work well and getting paid for it. Few call center managers recognize the outstanding potential that exists in their environment. A world of creativity is automatically built into the call center business. The environment, from the seats lined up in a row to management walking around motivating, is extremely conducive to inventiveness. Agents working on the telephone inside the office are a captive audience to a management team that must be creative and eclectic to keep them motivated.

Therefore, it is important for management to build a communication culture that embraces bells and whistles. Management should institute games, banners and sirens. (Literally! Playing cards, hanging signs and using bells are an appropriate form of communication in the call center.) Because agents are captive to the telephone, they feel stifled and require their management team to be empathetic towards their feelings and the difficulties of their daily job. Agents want attention. They want to know that their hard work is being noted. Agents want contests, awards, prizes, surprises. Agents are a much more creative and articulate group of individuals than are other types of employees. Therefore, the call center has a built-in opportunity to exploit the communication culture. Like their agents, management must be unique.

Have you ever sat in a room and watched the dynamic of a group of agents in progress? Speech is the communication of choice. People can talk! If management takes the necessary steps, the call center and its employees have the ability to become a wonderland of communication culture. Here is a simple analogy to consider. Creative minds in our society have made something as simple as a sporting event a very entertaining evening of fun and excitement. (Remember when the Super Bowl was simply considered just another game?) Today, the Super Bowl is a passionate, emotional, constructive bundle of communication culture. In addition, in the world of advertising, unique minds have taken the simplicity of a television commercial and turned the way messages are delivered upside down. Advertising has taken us from sales pitches in the 1960's and 1970's to unusual sales stories today. Commercial advertising today begins with stories, not sales pitches. In Southern California, Jack-in-the-Box has ongoing stories about "Jack" and his "jack balls". These stories are entertaining, visually pleasing and fun. The 10-20 commercials about "Jack" and his "jack balls" have become a fantastic staple of television advertising. The question is simple. Why can't call center managers bring the creativity of stories, messaging and symbols to the call center? The answer is that they can!

The best call center executives can take a page from these examples to build their own truly dynamic world. Through passionate communication culture, executives can make their call centers the super bowls of operations. They can turn daily operations into daily stories. Management must make the commitment to perform above and beyond the norms of creativity. They must see the potential that exists to boost performance objectives, and to boost agent opportunities. Agents will break records in call centers when management recognizes that call center performance is cultivated through *superior communication channels* which involve agents and their opinions. If you want your performance to improve, it means spending time in development and implementation in order to form superior communication channels. Channels may include meetings, one-on-one encounters, newsletters, voice mail, e-mail, letters, etc. Agents will exceed goals in every measurable area when management recognizes that they must establish a *culture in the call center that emphasizes agent input and opportunities.*

In general, the workplace is in a sad state of affairs because we place work before life. Executives forget that agents don't just come to work—they go to a second home. (In some cases, a first home). Many may not make the most money in the call center. Many may not have the best professional or educational background. Yet, all good agents own a passion, understanding and commitment to their call center as valuable as your own. The culture that management establishes may include the creation of management development teams, or weekly contests and awards. Above all else, however, the commitment to create a fantastic communication culture begins with those at the top.

To begin the process of creating passionate communication culture, take a moment and answer the following questions. Each question centers around finding out what is working well, or poorly, within your communication culture. The purpose of these questions is to get you to think about and understand the core of your communication culture. As you acknowledge each question, I want you to step away from providing the easy answers to the simple problems you can see and touch each day. Those solutions and challenges are easy. Instead, search for answers that provide meaning and are creative. Attempt to create answers that go to the core of your call center.

1. How does your management team administer operations on a daily basis? Describe communication standards as they exist among management, their peers and their agents.
2. How does your environment affect your call center agents?
3. Who are the management leaders that 1) Establish and 2) Implement strong communication channels on behalf of your agents? Do they separate themselves from other management personnel? Why?

4. What aspects of your call center would you call world class? Describe them and explain what is special about each one.

5. Which areas of your call center supply agents with clear opportunities to participate?

6. What are some of the steps management takes to promote communication between agents and management?

7. How would you rank management in terms of the following: Coaching agents.

   Listening to agents.

   Encouraging feedback from agents.

   Developing skill sets of agents.

8. How often do agents participate in decisions?

9. When was the last time your call center attempted to build a new culture? What was the result?

As you observe the operation of your call center, watch your managers and administrative staff as they conduct their daily duties. Have you ever noticed that most of their work centers around one another? Even most call center executives who truly interact with their agents still embody a sense of "me before they." Those managers, literally and symbolically, are not creating a communication culture that will ensure success. If you were to take your supervisors and administrative staff aside and ask them what their jobs are, chances are that not one would answer that their jobs are to create a tremendous communication culture in the call center on behalf of their agents. People don't think that way! They may say that they manage people, train people, support people and create an environment to meet and exceed performance standards. While those are all accurate answers, those answers are not enough to generate the best possible call center.

Let me give you some common examples of poor communication culture in the call center:

1. An administrative assistant works to support the call center floor. She is a conduit of communication between agents and staff. Her job is to support agents, but she doesn't see it that way. Clearly, agents get more done when she is most helpful. Yet, this administrative assistant sees agents as barriers to getting her work completed. She puts up signs directing agents to go elsewhere when she is busy completing an important assignment. She doesn't recognize that agents are her first priority. She complains to others when agents ask her for assistance.

2. A supervisor wants to monitor agent calls. He also wishes to spend time motivating his group. However, he finds his time is disrupted with re-

ports and paperwork. His agents come to him often for help on various issues, but he begs their forgiveness and asks them to come back at a later date so he can complete his project. He knows his first priority is his staff, but he recognizes the penalties if he doesn't complete his other projects. His other projects are deemed more important.

3. A senior executive is losing her sense of what is going on in her call center, and she can't help but enjoy her job more and more because of it. When she first began working in this call center, she was intimately involved with everything going on. Slowly, her duties caused her to drift away from operations, and her subordinates picked up the slack. In today's world, she is busy in meetings and planning sessions that directly involve her call center, but she is beginning to forget the names of various agents, and where they sit. Agents who began working for the company two years ago are still considered "new" in her mind.

What you read above is typical of many call center organizations. Management becomes engrossed in its duties at the expense of the employees. Yet most managers don't want this to be the case. They understand that they need to address their agents more. They simply have lost sight of how to begin implementation.

Desire + Concept + Initiative = Communication Culture

Let's take a step back for a moment and address the core fundamentals of implementing communication culture. The concept begins with a three step process. Its premise is simple. Management's *desire* to build a fantastic communication culture, coupled with management's *concept* of what that communication culture can embody, may only come to fruition when both management and staff gain the *initiative* to develop and consummate a new communication culture. In effect, desire must exist for a concept to materialize. Yet, desire and concept mean nothing if call center managers, supervisors and agents don't posses the initiative to make it happen.

My experience has been that most call center management has a penchant towards *desire*. That means they have the desire to create something better than what presently exists. They may not have the time, resources or skills to do so, but their intentions are good. I am often called in to create new communication culture because somebody possessed the desire to retain my services. This desire might involve anything needed, from telesales training to organizational management. This desire constitutes merely the seed to a creation, not the creation itself. You don't build a house without having the desire to create a house. Desire propels us forward. It leads to a foundation. In many call centers, perhaps yours, all levels of management, as well as agents, have the desire to implement something new or different. Their passion may wane as time progresses. It may peak or valley depending on a million different circumstances. But in most call centers, at the core, the desire to build, create, mold and facilitate something, from a simple proposal to a thrilling new communication culture, does exist.

My experience has also shown that senior management tends to lack the correct *concepts* to create the best communication culture possible. In fact, isn't it funny that frontline agents usually have the majority of terrific concepts as to how to build a communication culture? For example, pluck five agents from the telephone and tell them to be creative, and dozens of concepts will be offered. Those concepts may not be practical, but ideas pop up far more often at the bottom of the food chain than at the top. That is because as the food chain goes down, the opportunity to consistently create and propose on a regular basis goes down as well. Therefore, hundreds of fantastic proposals lie unused and unsolicited, because nobody is asking the agents their opinions. (If every person has fifty ideas, yet only senior executives are allowed to propose ideas, then eventually senior executives will have no ideas left, and each non-executive will still have his fifty.) Clearly, management wants to meet goals and please customers. Often they are so busy with structure, however, that they lack the understanding of how to do so. Their concepts are stale. They see the call center through the prism of their own eyes, not necessarily the way the rest of the call center sees itself. As a result, the organization suffers. It isn't because management can't create communication culture if given the right tools. It isn't because they don't have the desire or talent to do so. It is usually because they haven't embraced concepts as they relate to the entire company. Ideas, proposals and suggestions are the cornerstones of any powerful communication culture. They are the cornerstones to any successful corporation. Management must understand that concepts create their opportunities. Management must realize that agents are usually the entities that possess all the creative concepts.

> The great challenge in building communication culture is that it involves human emotions, human thoughts and human feelings.

Finally, *initiative* is the battle that rarely gets won. The building of a communication culture generally dies because the initiative to make it happen wilts. A management team may have the time to implement ten concepts next year, yet there may be thirty concepts available to implement. Who has the initiative to execute even the ten best? Management rallies troops in the desire to be world class. They create magnificent concepts with regard to how to make it a reality. Then, they falter. They don't close the sale. They can't seal the deal. They can't bring thoughts and actualities to realization. They can't implement the concepts. Management runs out of energy, loses focus, gets frustrated over barriers, or moves on to what they consider to be more pressing issues. The inability to maintain initiative is the foremost reason why call centers fail to create a performance-based communication culture.

Building Channels of Communication in the Call Center

The ability to effectively communicate involves sending messages through an assortment of channels. Therefore, if one person communicates to a group of fifty, there is a channel that carries messages from that one person to each of those fifty people. If appropriate, communication is returned from each of those fifty people to that one person. Those channels may constitute a meeting or an overhead display. In addition, various noises impact the channel of communication between one person and another. Noise may include opinions, comments, actions and outside influences.

I have listed some channels of communication within the context of the call center. From modern day technology to century old processes, each aspect has pros and cons. Some channels of communication come with various elements of noise. Some have no noise, but may not impact the communication culture of a call center as well as others. Every channel of communication can play an intricate role in developing fabulous communication culture for your call center.

1. E-Mail
2. Instant Messages
3. Voice Mail
4. Intranet
5. One-on-one Communication
6. Team Communication
7. Off-Site Meetings
8. Company Meetings
9. Overhead Projector
10. White Board
11. Easel Pad
12. Personal Memos
13. Group Memos
14. Personal Fliers

15. Group Fliers
16. Internet
17. You
18. GOSSIP!!!!!!!!

The channels of communication that management may utilize are endless. Yet for some reason, management does not use many of these channels in order to facilitate communication culture. They could if they so chose, but they generally don't, for a myriad of reasons. Those reasons almost always begin with a lack of *desire, concept or initiative.*

Let me give you an example of how easy it can be for any call center to implement some of these communication channels. At one call center that staffed fifty agents each shift, management agreed that we were going to communicate a consistent and central message to our agents when they walked in for work each day. We had the *desire* to do better than we were doing when it involved delivering early morning messages. Our communication at the time was haphazard and non-existent, and we were not using communication to build a strong communication culture. Hence, our performance was lagging. A consistent and central message was required to set the tone for the entire shift. After a meeting in which we explored various *concepts*, including identifying what we wanted to accomplish, we were in agreement that the message would be displayed each and every day in the same part of the call center on an overhead projector. The message would communicate the following points:

1. How the entire group performed the previous day.
2. Expectations for the group today.
3. The motivation and communication they should expect to receive from their supervisors this day.
4. Any other relevant information.

Our goal was to condition our agents to go to the same place each day for valuable messages. By doing so, we could ensure that our agents would gain useful information consistently in order for them to become more successful employees. We wanted to build our call center into a culture of opportunity. For instance, sometimes we placed happy birthday wishes on the overhead display. Other times, we commended outstanding performances from agents. Additionally, we provided updated competitor news and listed information on the comings and goings of our staff. Our agents knew where to find daily information; our management staff knew how and where to communicate daily information.

We also wanted to bring consistency to the way management communicated and agents received that communication. By doing this, we would have the complete attention of our agents, and our agents would become, over time, anticipatory toward our messages because they knew something of interest would be communicated. It was a great way to start the day! The best part of this process is that it motivated management to become organized. Once a week, senior management would stand at the overhead projector like tour guides, commenting on one or two areas of interest. Other days, shift supervisors might be present with food such as donuts or sodas, or handouts such as memos and booklets.

We had the *desire* to successfully create positive communication culture in the call center. We outlined a *concept* of what we wished to accomplish so we had clear objectives. Objectives included: 1) We wanted to have a consistent and effective form of communication to start each day; 2) We wanted the agents to condition themselves to observe and understand this form of communication so they could use it to their advantage on the telephones; 3) We wanted to build a culture of opportunity around this communication that brought together agents, management and senior management; 4) We wanted to demonstrate to our agents that we had the desire and initiative to replicate this project and build new opportunities in the call center for them; and 5) We wanted management to become organized in their communication habits. It took our staff less than thirty minutes to devise the initial game plan, and over time we adapted and changed our project to achieve maximum effectiveness.

The key to this whole process of communication culture was *initiative*. If we had gone our separate ways, the *desire* and *concept* that built this idea would have been wasted. Each manager would have moved on to his central area for the day, and nobody would have engendered the initiative to make it happen. Fortunately, assignments were duly handed out, and the project went off without a hitch. In this scenario, *desire + concept + initiative did equal success*. Management developed alternative communication methods to communicate with our call center agents. It wasn't the same old talk to the group before the start of the day, and it wasn't a bland memorandum with a "read the memo" message. In addition, management set a tone for the day that carried over to all agents. Supervisors structured their day based on the themes outlined on the overhead projector, and their communication of those themes built a climate for the day that helped every staff member achieve goals. The entire call center had a mission, and that mission was plainly communicated. Most valuable was the conditioning of the agents. It became priceless. How hard is it to get fifty agents to do the same thing, all at once? Pretty tough! It's difficult enough keeping fifty agents on-line when the queue is backed up, or on the telephone when the outbound dialer is dialing a weak area. To top that, how much harder is it to make all fifty agents do the same thing at once because they want to do it and because they enjoy it?

Communication Culture is the foundation, daily practice, structure and philosophy of your call center operation. In your call center today, you have a form of communication culture. It motivates performance. It impacts attitudes, decision making, retention. *It is not nearly what it can be*. Communication Culture can literally bring a focus and energy to your call center that you may deem impossible today. Agents and supervisors respond. Senior management gets results. Retention improves. It involves hard work and a detailed plan. Most importantly, it involves *desire + concept + initiative*.

CHAPTER 5

How Call Center Agents View The Call Center

"Find a job that you love and you'll never work a day in your life."
John P. Grier

Management must take time to analyze how call center agents view their world in order to build a world class communication culture. It's not an understatement to say that management's perception of the call center and the way agents view it is quite different from what agents perceive. For instance, an analyst once asked a senior executive why agents in his call center didn't turn over as rapidly as the industry average. Retention was fantastic. The executive said "Because we provide an outstanding management team and we pay better than the competition." However, when the analyst sampled the agents, their consensus was a little different. "Management doesn't pay attention to extra lunches, leaving early and coming in late. We go and come as we wish. Plus, at the moment, they are the only game in town."

Mediocre management looks at call centers through their own prisms. They see their world as one that can be impacted based on their decisions. They make decisions on seating arrangements, project assignments, compensation, policies and procedures, contests, etc, based on their assessments. Agents understand that management does this, and it bothers them immeasurably. In lunch meetings, break conversations and after work, agents talk to one another about how management makes decisions without bringing agents in the loop. In essence, management "makes decisions without consulting us on what is really going on."

How Agents View The Call Center

Below, I have listed twenty-one areas with respect to the way agents observe the call center.

1. A majority of call center agents recognize that first-level supervisors have little decision-making capability. They understand that first-level

supervisors are squeezed between upper management and themselves. This opinion by agents is reinforced when they receive a "no" answer from the first-level supervisor and a "yes" response from the less-exposed senior executive. Agents know that upper management makes final decisions, and first line supervisors enforce those decisions. Yet, the communication from the front line supervisor to the agents is the one the agents take most seriously. Why? Because, the front line supervisor is the person the agent has the most direct contact with. The agent receives pay raises, performance reviews and consistent interpersonal communication from the front line supervisor. The channel of communication usually stops at this level. The agent's trust and confidence are with the front line supervisor. Yet, when it comes to *decision-making capability*, agents understand that their supervisor is simply in parrot mode. Agents recognize that supervisors provide answers based on what they have been provided, not based on their own choices or opinions. Therefore, agents know that final decisions rest at levels above their supervisors.

> Agents recognize that upper management makes final decisions and front line supervisors enforce those decisions. Agents understand that if they can't get results from their immediate supervisor, they can go up to the next level.

Although agents see their supervisors as their main line of contact, agents will not hesitate to use their supervisors' boss to get what they need. One can see an analogy with children and their parents. A child may ask one parent if he may go to the ice cream shop. When that parent says "no", the child goes to the next parent, who now has the position of wielding more power. Because of the conditioning they received as children, agents in the call center have perceived that going from supervisor to supervisor's boss works! They learned as kids that it works, so they use the same game in the working world. One of the great travesties of supervisor-agent management is that the higher agents go up the management ladder, the more likely some high-level executive with little knowledge of the actual situation will make the wrong decision. (How many times does parent B tell parent A, "I thought it was okay to give her the candy bar.") In so many work environments, supervisors make a decision, agents appeal above the supervisor, and the decision is repealed. Supervisors lose all credibility, and agents learn a new way to manipulate decisions in their call center. One agent told me "When I need something important done, I go above my supervisor to her manager, because he always gets it done for me." Although agents understand the quandary first-level supervisors are in, they are not sympathetic towards it. In fact, one must expect agents to exploit the decision-making ladder when supervisors make a decision which agents don't appreciate. Also, one must expect the more savvy and veteran agents to use their supervisor's lack of power to their advantage at critical junctures. Agents are intelligent enough not to exploit their advantage every time—just when they need it. This is the communication culture that exists in thousands of call centers across the world.

2. Call Center agents who work for service agencies view the call center as ever-changing. For instance, a very small percentage of call centers have limited turnover. Most call centers find that one of their top challenges is facing continuous turnover from their agent staff, management, and clients. Many service agencies that handle accounts for clients turn over their agents, first line supervisors and support staff faster than one could ever imagine, and in today's world I am sure we all can imagine quite a bit. This turnover isn't a knock on service agencies, but merely a result of a changing industry. Agents who work for large call center agencies have come to expect that clients might come and go, and, to the same degree, jobs may come and go as well. They don't want this to happen, and they may or may not understand *why* it happens, but they recognize that it does happen. Therefore, agents who work for service agencies have learned not to rely on long-term commitments from management or peers or clients, because over a period of months they have probably witnessed turnover in the management, peers and clients that existed when they began their jobs. In turn, they tend not to provide long term commitments as well.

3. Agents expect compensation to change for the worse. Agents fear change in finances. Agents believe that a compensation change is never for the better, because most call centers make compensation changes to better the business, not the agent. Certainly, changes have been instituted for the better, but agents expect the worst when a new compensation plan is introduced. If given the choice, agents by and large would value the opportunity to keep compensation steady.

4. More than anything, agents desire an appealing communication culture. Call center agents want to work somewhere other than the boiler room next door. The world-class call center that has a world-class environment can build terrific employee retention, even when they may not pay the most, or offer the best benefits. Comfortable surroundings matter!

5. Call Center agents desire a business that has a proven track record. Make no mistake about the fact that having proven management,

guidelines, policies, and a successful track record can make all the difference in the effort to retain call center agents. Consistency is extremely important. New call centers that begin their operations correctly can display a proven track record through the people who relish their jobs. Veteran call centers that have never done their job right may never be able to show their employees a proven track record, regardless of years spent trying. This lack of consistency and success stands out when new agents apply for positions.

6. Call Centers must exceed the competition. In some cities, call centers face fierce competition for employees. Agents hop around from company to company at the same pace as blackjack dealers move about in Las Vegas. Many agents move around for better pay, but not all. In most surveys about call center agents, more pay has never been the number one factor in job switching. A better place to work has been at or near the top. Pay is usually an addendum to that, but not the sole reason why agents job hop.

7. The call center must provide growth and adaptability. Some call center agents want to try something new and leave companies that have zero growth. Other agents relish their positions, but would like to contribute more. Agents look for call centers that treat the employee better. The question you may have is: "Better than whom?" That answer is irrelevant. Agents want "better" versus the past experiences each individual has had at one time or another.

> Agents who work for large call center agencies have come to expect that clients might come and go, and, to the same degree, jobs may come and go as well.

8. Steady management makes a huge difference. Agents dislike breaking in new supervisors. They want to develop a strong bond with their supervisor, and starting over with a new one constitutes a setback for them. They feel the supervisor they have knows how to work with them best.

9. Agents desire fair resolutions to disagreements. In some cases, this is a subjective request. What is fair for one may not always be fair for the other. Yet, successful firms, particularly sales firms, thrive off competition. The thing that always arrives with competition is arbitration. Management is called in to arbitrate a variety of avenues in the call center, from sales distribution and ownership to fair practices.

10. Agents desire extensive training and residual training (new hire training, product training, sales training). One of the questions potential new hires ask in interviews is whether there is training for the position. If so, is it paid, and how long does it last. The answers to those questions provide a big commentary on the company. Call Centers

that provide little or no training, or don't pay their agents to go through training, tend to not be worthy of a quality agent's time and effort. In addition, the best call center not only trains, but provides residual training to increase an agent's skill level.

11. Agents hope for call centers that provide some opportunity to advance. Not all agents desire to move up in the organization, or within the organization. However, basic management dictates that organizations which provide career opportunities and room to advance have a much more dedicated and strengthened work force than those organizations that don't. In the call center, sitting on the telephone constantly can be so repetitive that the challenge dissipates. Quality agents who can contribute more than just working on the telephone need to be provided an outlet to do so.

12. Call Center agents hope their management unit will listen to and think about problems before acting. Management can sometimes find itself reacting to issues and concerns without first taking the time to listen completely to what those issues and concerns are, and how best to handle them. For instance, agents tend to use their supervisors to vent, but they don't want any action taken. Oftentimes, the supervisor should take a step back and say "Is this something you want me to act upon?"

13. Agents desire their call center to be "fair". This is another subjective wish, but certainly one that holds validity. What does "fair" mean to the agent? Usually, it revolves around making decisions involving two or more agents. In many roundtables, agents will speak of how they left organizations because management wasn't fair to agents as a whole, or played favorites with one agent over another.

14. Agents want a management team that is empathetic. All veteran agents I have met have remained working for their supervisor because the supervisor clearly cares for them as people as well as workers. It is very challenging to find quality supervisors who are empathetic to their agents and their agents' situations.

15. Agents observe their product as it relates to the market. They want a product that is on the "up and up". In the world of telesales, there are quite a few programs and businesses that don't compete with their competition. There are more that compete, but not in a legitimate fashion. If an agent wants to work for one of those firms, then management shouldn't want that agent working for them.

16. Agents appreciate a call center that maintains a balance between discipline and flexibility. In one job I had, every agent I managed told me, a minimum of one time, that they were pleased with the fact that I would okay them to leave early if they asked. At the same time, those agents were the same ones who made sure to alert me to any

extra time they took at lunch or breaks, so I could "dock" their time card if applicable. Management has the impression that agents try to "get away" with as much as they can. In some instances, that is true. However, usually agents truly desire the balance of discipline with flexibility. Similar to children, they don't want to be given everything they have ever wanted, because they desire limits combined with fairness and empathy.

17. Agents desire rules that are clear and easy to understand. For management, the hardest part of developing rules is that those rules may not be clear to the people who actually work with them: the agents.

18. Agents desire rules in writing that maintain consistency. I have been part of call centers that changed the same rule over and over again. "What is today's edict on this rule?" I sometimes asked. Inconsistency with regard to the rules and regulations of a game breeds poor players. Can you imagine a basketball player who doesn't know whether a 3-point shot will actually count for 3 points? Or, a baseball player who doesn't realize that for this week only, there are four outs in an inning?

19. Agents desire rules that are enforced. In many cases, policies and procedures are words with no foundation. Veteran agents have probably worked for call centers that had comprehensive rules for every issue, until it came time to enforce those issues. Then, management subjectivity came into play. A consensus among agents is that they respect rules that are enforced, even when the rule goes against them. "As long as it works both ways, I am fine with it" is a phrase I have heard over and over again.

> In some cities, call centers face fierce competition for employees. Agents hop around from company to company at the same pace as blackjack dealers move about in Las Vegas.

20. Agents hope the call center employs technology that is easy to use and convenient. One of the greatest agent fears is inability to master technology. Technology is meant to simplify work in the call center, but sometimes it adds more angst than ease to the agent's daily environment. New agents, in particular, almost always question the type of technology that exists in the call center, and how cumbersome that technology is to orchestrate.

21. Agents react favorably to call centers that provide games, excitement, and motivation. When agents see a call center, they see the fun. Prizes, contests, energy. If your agent walks up to you and says "We need something exciting around here," you can be sure he is tuned in to motivation.

A Call Center As A School

Agents see their jobs in the call center as an extension of school. Supervisors see that relationship as well. School is a symbol all employees can relate with because everybody who works in the call center has lived through the experience of school years. Supervisors have been known to use the analogy that their agents are school kids when they talk about their agents to management peers. Using sentences such as "My kids are doing great" or "The kids are loose again" or "Alright group, it's nap time" or "Alright everyone, playtime is over with", supervisors can recall from past experience how their roles mimic the roles of teachers. The meaning of supervisors equating agents to school kids is not to demean the intelligence of the agents. Rather, it is to emphasize the similarities of a familiar situation that everybody, from supervisor to agent, can relate to.

The thought process between call center and school parallels. For instance, in school we can all probably recall cliques that formed in order to create each individual's atmosphere and experience. The same in call centers. Supervisors must recognize that agents bond differently with one another based on a multitude of factors. Remember how in school we each ate in lunch groups? Usually, those groups were somewhat familiar. Agents treat lunch the same way. Remember how in school we liked some parts of the day, some classes, and some teachers, but not others? Agents view the call center the same way. For instance, agents may dislike taking member service calls from Alabama, but love taking calls from Oregon. Agents may dislike one supervisor, but value the intelligence and input of another. And agents may dislike making outbound telesales calls to prospects before 10:00am, but love to do so after 2:00pm. School involved a team of people and a leader who provided direction. The call center as a "school" analogizes very nicely.

In all parts of society, we relate one instance to another instance because both instances are familiar. When a new agent walks into a call center, he sees himself as the new kid walking into the classroom. Agents see, subliminally and outright, the relationship of their work environment to the relationships they had while growing up in school. School is what agents know and understand. It is a safe period of time when their responsibility was to work and learn while the teachers and administration dealt with the challenges of operations. The results are very telling. Agents who had been gossip artists in high school carry that practice over to the call center. Those agents can very well be channels of communication which supervisors use to control their environment. (Why send a memo when you can use Joan to carry the message?) Agents who were shy and introverted in the group scene in high school also tend to portray shy and introverted qualities in the group environment in the call center. And those that snacked on pretzels in class are usually the ones you can expect to snack on pretzels at work.

I believe it is important for supervisors to take a snapshot of consistent themes between call centers and schools and create images to help them understand what agents see when they observe their call center. For instance, let's take the snapshot of "structure" as it relates to both call centers and school.

STRUCTURE AS IT RELATES TO CALL CENTERS AND SCHOOL		
	CALL CENTER	**SCHOOL**
Start at certain time	X	X
Finish at certain time	X	X
Consistent lunch and breaks	X	X
Consistent teacher / superv.	X	X
Consistent curriculum	X	X
Consistent environment	X	X
Consistent turnover	X	X
Guest speakers	X	X
New subjects and topics	X	X
Upper management / Principal	X	X
Network of friends / enemies	X	X
Exams, goals, lesson plans	X	X
Emotions and Relationships	X	X
Outside factors that influence	X	X
Culture and environment	X	X

This list could probably be endless. But telling. A successful call center, just like a successful school, finds itself with the same organizational philosophy. They both are finely tuned machines that predicate themselves on a strong foundation of structure. Agents and students are not finely tuned machines and they don't predicate themselves on structure. Therefore, the call center and school must provide the framework. For example, perhaps customer care agents are required to staff a shift from 11:00pm to 7:00am. From management's view, it is impractical for agents to disappear for three hours in the middle of the shift. And, if students are mandated to be in class from 8:00am to 3:00pm, it is impractical for a whole class of students to disappear for three hours in the middle of their school day. Yet, agents see their call center through the prism of their view of school. The impractical can and does become practical. We all remember when students ditched class, took longer lunches and breaks, and gained advantage from any and all loopholes in the structure. Our call center agents do the same because they have been taught to do the same. Students viewed school as a structured entity that they could, in various fashions, manipulate. Agents view the call center in the exact same way.

Call Centers Should Take A Page From Schools

Schools are beginning to embrace changes that allow students to see their institution in a positive light. Many schools now condone their seniors leaving campus for lunch, or allow seniors to take an extra hour for lunch instead of one hour or less. Many schools have allowed class acceleration. Students who wish to graduate a semester early may do so. Or, some students are allowed to start school an hour later, or perhaps end an hour earlier, or drop a class time (usually the last class of the day) for an entire year. Many schools have moved from the semester system to the quarter system and the year-round school system. In addition, schools emphasize more electives today than ever before. Schools have added more multi-cultural clubs and organizations than ever before. One example of the creativity I support wholeheartedly is making gains throughout the country. Many schools take 10-15 minutes out of one class period to promote reading. Every day, all action stops and everybody in school reads. What a great idea! Imagine what would happen in your call center if every day, work stopped for 10-15 minutes, and all employees would be required to do nothing but read? (I remember a class I took in junior high school that was called "reading for pleasure". For the entire 50 minute class, students read an assortment of books, magazines and newspapers, and turned in synopsis reports about it. Great idea!)

School is a symbol all employees can relate with because everybody who works in the call center has lived through the experience of school years.

Schools are beginning to change the framework we remember in the hope that this change will foster student growth. In some cities, students now see their school as one of opportunity. It would be wise for call centers to do the same.

CHAPTER 6

Grappling With Emotions
In The Call Center

*"Remember that a person's name is to that person the
sweetest and most important
sound in any language."*
Dale Carnegie

We have identified that a world class communication culture is the preeminent way to create call center operations. At its peak, it makes your call center stand out from all the rest, and exceed all imaginable performance standards. We have also touched upon the value that agents place in a quality call center. Agent feelings and desires are perhaps the most forgotten aspect of call center management. Building on those two premises, one can begin to build a positive communication culture with recognition that communication culture and agent performance are by-products of human emotions. The way we communicate is a by-product of how we want to communicate at any particular time. Emotions play a supreme role in creating that base. Perhaps we are thrilled over a week of excellent call handling, or a month of solid sales production. Besides facts and figures, our communication is developed from and presented through our emotions; games, thank-you messages, award certificates, motivational speeches. In addition, how we create culture and implement culture is also based on our emotions. Inventiveness is an emotional attribute, not a logical attribute. Most of the truly creative minds throughout our society are creative based upon their emotional juices to be so — their desire to be creative. It's not a surprise that in a job that demands very creative performers, telesales agents and customer service agents thrive on emotions to help them succeed everyday. The impact that emotions play stands out as one of the most critical arenas. Agents become motivated based on how they recognize and utilize their emotions, and how they receive emotional vibes from their supervisors. In addition, management motivates agents based on their own ability to understand their own emotions. Decisions are not always made based purely on data. Indeed, emotions are the foundation for many decisions. Although management wishes to believe that decisions and successes are based on practicality and reasoning, not emotions, call centers simply don't work that way. The people who succeed day-in and day-out are those folks who have an understanding of the role emotions play.

When we discuss emotions, we discuss an intangible. The subjective comes into play. If an agent makes twenty sales in a month against a goal of eleven, can we attribute the extra nine sales to emotions? Can a customer service team that manages to diffuse a threatening issue thank emotions as the reason for success? Are negative emotions by agents and management always a threat to performance? Can superior communication culture thrive when emotions are always foremost? When management makes decisions, are they making those decisions based on well thought-out practices, or merely on emotional desires? How much do management's emotions factor in when management goes about motivating agents? When agents have problems, how much of a factor does emotion play in their attitudes and opinions?

Agents become motivated based on how they manage emotions to benefit their job.

Each question elicits a different answer from different parties. Ten managers answer ten different ways, and thirty-five agents provide thirty-five interesting yet different responses. There is no correct answer, nor is there meant to be a correct answer. Yet what is very clear is that the emotional patterns by management and agents clearly dominate communication culture. If I had a dollar for each time a supervisor or team lead communicated to me utilizing their emotions first, I would be a billionaire. If I had a resume' for every call center agent who used emotions to explain why they are disappointed at work, I could start my own recruiting service nationwide. If I could sell one book for each senior executive or manager who lost control of their emotions and mouthed off in a meeting without thinking first, I will have sold enough books to be in the top five on Amazon.com. Losing control of one's emotions can damage superior communication culture between operations, management, and agents. Using emotions without recognizing that emotions are commanding the performance can also set call center culture back if actions are taken based purely on those emotions. Have you ever been in a meeting when the senior executive flies off the handle, demands action, threatens security, and puts all involved on pins and needles? Whether his emotional outburst is warranted or not, the real danger around his emotional outburst is that his subordinates will follow the example, lead via his verbatim pleas, and bring more innocent bystanders into the emotional loop. I have been on the receiving end of emotional reactions, and my emotional reactions have at times taken months of well-planned communication culture and destroyed it.

Of course, emotions are not always detrimental to communication culture.

For instance, when a telesales agent reaches nine sales in a day and her goal is ten, she will do anything her emotions allow her to do in order to make that tenth sale. It may not be logical for her to be excited and focused for merely one sale. However, her emotions have told her that this one sale now holds more importance to her than the first nine. She is dedicated to meeting her goal of ten! And look at her personality and spirit after making that tenth sale! She's through the roof with happiness. Although each one of her nine sales played an equal role in helping her achieve ten sales, it was the momentum and objective to reach that tenth sale that made her day a complete success. I have walked up to agents who accomplished this very feat. I have asked "Why weren't you as excited about sale six, or sale two, or sale eight?" I do not do this to stop her excitement, but merely to watch the gleam in her eyes and smile on her face as she says "Come on Dan, those aren't as important as this one. This is ten!" Here is another example. After a customer service agent spends thirty minutes assisting a customer, that agent is tired and drained—but emotionally pleased. Nine times out of ten, that agent is more likely to *want* to take another call soon. One agent has told me over and over again that spending a long time with one customer "Is the fun part of the job. Getting off the telephone with them after they know they are going to get what they want is what makes this job worthwhile."

We can take an example from professional athletics to understand how emotions challenge and impact communication culture in the call center. In professional athletics, emotions encompass a huge part of the playing experience. Players channel their positive emotions to give them second efforts on the court. When a basketball team scores 12 straight points and they are on a roll, they continue to channel their emotions forward because of their adrenaline. The crowd keeps them pumped up. They feel good. Their head coach implores them to keep pushing, keep winning, keep trying, and players take the encouragement most readily because they are winning. In football, when a team needs an emotional boost from their fans, the players raise their arms to the crowd, in an uplifting gesture. The players want the fans to become emotional, so the players will become more emotional. Football players know that a vast percentage of their game is predicated upon a pure emotional rush. Because of emotions, players do things on the football field that they would never do off. Emotions do not affect only those teams and players that win, either. Players are fighting against the tide when they are losing, and they feel as if the emotional balloon has burst. They need to do anything they can to overcome the tide. Their lack of adrenaline and their negative emotions pull them down. The crowd booing against them depresses them. They need a break to move forward. They need an emotional upswing. Teams in this position must win two or three games in a row. Players must sink four or five baskets to break away from the negative emotions.

Emotions impact everything in the call center. The call center, to function in a superior way, must be understood first as an emotional medium. Perhaps you have peers around you today who see the call center as a statistical world, a business world, and a production or service world. Those folks miss the boat. You need to show them why. Those folks try to hold their agents to textbook standards, even if it means ignoring every aspect of human emotions. Those folks haven't understood how superior communication culture in any industry, from sports to sales to member service, makes operations thrive. They don't see why sports teams win fifteen games in a row, and why sports teams lose fifteen games in a row. They don't recognize how truly emotional the world of the call center is for the participants who are responsible to ensure the call center expands and breaks performance goals. If the call center consisted of robots and computers, emotions wouldn't play any factor. As much as managing robots and computers would make the life of a supervisor much simpler, it doesn't happen that way. People manage people, and emotions are the barometer that sets the table.

Let me provide an example of a typical emotional experience that occurs in any telesales unit. As a call center manager, you may see an agent who has broken his career high in sales with a super sales performance. A manager who does not understand the value of emotions will do nothing. A manager who recognizes how emotions can create and dictate successful performance then rewards that agent through efforts such as verbal congratulations, prizes and department recognition. Quality managers understand they must make it a point of taking a successful event and building on that successful event for the benefit of the agent and the entire department. The manager may say "Great job, you did awesome, you must feel fantastic for hitting your high in sales!" The manager might then go around to his peers and let them know, in a raised voice so all can hear, how well that agent did today. "Can you believe Bill broke XYZ sales today? He's unbelievable!" The manager may sense how emotions can truly help Bill and the entire department, so he may go back to Bill and tell him to take an extra thirty minutes for lunch tomorrow so he can enjoy his accomplishment. In the process of this two-minute interaction, Bill is thrilled, motivated and confident because he has achieved a new standard, and that new standard has been recognized by his supervisor. His positive emotions are at an all time high. He feels great about himself, his results, his department, his company. If you took a survey of Bill today, he would rate areas such as call center climate, manager skills, pay and enjoyment of work extremely high. Most relevant is the fact that Bill doesn't want to get off the telephone right now. Bill wants to get to work the next day as early as possible. The manager probably couldn't drag Bill away from the telephone if he had a buffet full of food down the hall. In essence, the manager who understands how to use emotions to his advantage can make a

> A call center with little energy and the feeling of "zero success" is a call center trickling toward death.

positive for one day turn into a positive for many days. The manager can create opportunities for his employees and department. That is his job.

Let's explore further how this manager can manipulate emotions to his advantage. In addition to Bill feeling good, his peers feel good about quite a few things, as well. First, they feel good that their supervisor cares enough about his staff to walk around and take time to congratulate employees for a job well done. I am not entirely certain that agents *know* they feel this way about their supervisor when he puts on a show on behalf of another agent, but they do. Other agents very often approach the supervisor and may communicate something to the affect of "That positive motivation keeps all of our emotions up." Second, they feel confident that they can earn results just like Bill did, if for no other reason than they want the attention that Bill received. Hearing that Bill has a career high in sales motivates other agents to do the same exact thing. They see it happen, and it gets emphasized by their supervisor, and now they know that it can happen for them, too. In almost 100% of instances, peers of Bill would not have recognized Bill had a career high in sales without the supervisor sharing the success. Even when sales numbers are posted each day on the wall, nobody but Bill and the supervisor would recognize what Bill's total numbers meant, and it usually isn't Bill who communicates his success to his peers. I don't know if agents *recognize* they want to hit their career high in sales so the supervisor will dote over them, but a large part of the motivational value of the prizes one person gets stems from the fact that another person wants the same thing. Third, in most other departments, supervisors don't walk around verbalizing success and handing out prizes for doing a job a bit above average. It doesn't need to be done that way, because those departments don't need emotions to keep them working and happy. Imagine what would happen if the supervisor of a department used emotions to motivate individuals and the department as a whole each time her administrative assistant typed a memo correctly? It would be ridiculous. Can you see a supervisor handing out prizes, ringing bells, announcing awards and hooting and hollering simply for a correct memo? Yet in the call center, this practice can become the standard. The call center presents itself as a place where motivation and excitement and management attention should take place regularly. In a later chapter, we will explore practical ways to make this happen.

> Management hopes that their executive decisions are based on practicality and reasoning, not emotions. This is simply not true.

The above examples touch upon emotions as a positive, and emotions are not always positive. Negative emotions can cripple a communication culture. Agents begin feeling something is wrong when they feel negative emotions in the environment; negative emotions from peers, outside influences, or management itself. And management is very often the cause and effect of negative communication in the call center. While positive emotions from supervisor to agent are an uplifting and motivational foundation under which agents thrive, negative emotions from supervisors to agents give agents an environment that works against them. This environment does nothing to help call center agents exploit their strengths. Here is a simple example I am certain call center supervisors can relate to. When management does positive things, one after another, there is a percentage of agents on the floor that take that motivation for granted, and don't even recognize it, much less appreciate it. A supervisor may therefore not believe that their positive communication is making an impact. Those agents have seemingly come to expect that management should create emotional positives. However, when management turns just a smidgen negative, those are the same agents who leap up to criticize supervisors for not providing quality motivation. Truth be told, supervisors have such a powerful influence on their agents that their very actions and words manipulate the actions of their agents. In athletics, the manager of a baseball team can bring his troops down and raise them up. For instance, when a sports team is in a downturn, the manager may call a team meeting and lambaste the team. This might be construed as negative emotions that bring the team further down, or it might be an emotional challenge that encourages the team to excel.

Call center supervisors face the same challenges. If a telesales department endures twelve days in a row of losing numbers, that department is in some fashion of trouble. If a baseball team has sixteen days in a row of losing games, that team is in some fashion of trouble. How does the baseball manager re-motivate his squad? How does he lay the foundation of positive emotions to keep his players focused on providing 100%? How does the supervisor meet those challenges as well? Supervisors must understand how their emotions and their reactions to the emotions around them affect communication culture.

> If I could sell one book for each senior executive or manager who lost their emotions in a meeting and made irrational decisions without thinking of the consequences, I will have sold enough books to be on the Amazon.com top five.

When agents are negative on the call center floor, the supervisor must get them away from the call center floor and into a place where they can channel their negative emotions away from their peers. When supervisors go negative, they too must channel those energies away from the floor. It is always okay to blow up over a situation — it is never okay to blow up over a situation in front of peers. *What* an agent is negative about may be extremely valid, and it should be addressed. *How* the agent is displaying his frustration shouldn't be presented to the entire group. People who find a reason to complain can get peers to follow suit. A fantastic day at work can turn negative in seconds because of the opinions and comments of one or two agents or supervisors. A premier communication culture will thereby be set back.

When one takes a walk around different departments of a major corporation, it is the call center that stands out separate from the rest. Human resources looks similar to accounting which looks similar to publicity which mimics the administrative area of the corporation. To the casual observer, the call center looks like a world completely out of place. All because of emotions. In every other department, the objective of supervisors is to ensure that employees get the job done. Emotions may exist at times. In the call center, one can expect to see supervisors running around clapping hands and motivating agents with shouts of encouragement. Bells might be ringing, music might be playing, prizes might be given away. Hitting a goal is not enough. Getting the job done well is only acceptable. In sales and member service, breaking records is encouraged and expected. In the call center, the noise level should be loud so it encourages *movement* and *expression*. In the process, the emotions of employees get stirred up. In other business departments, movement and expression may be synonymous with trouble. Competent quiet means work is getting done. In the call center, competent quiet is synonymous with trouble. When management walks into the call center, they should use their ears well before they use their eyes. A call center with low volume is a call center trickling toward death. No matter what the product, program, business, acoustics and objectives, a call center that sounds more like accounting than an amusement park is destined not to break records every day. Let your ears do the listening the next time you visit your call center. How does it sound? Do you hear laughing, enthusiasm and teamwork? If you do not, allow your eyes to show you why you might not. Look for the supervisors and see what they are doing. Glance at the walls and analyze the culture. Understand *movement* and *expression*. Recognize how emotions are playing with the communication culture.

> **Quality managers must understand they should take a successful event and build on that event for the benefit of the rest of the call center. By doing so, agents respond emotionally to the success of a peer.**

Good supervisors will use emotions in countless ways. When a telesales agent is clearly having a poor day, and is frustrated about it, the supervisor can use that person's "down" emotion to everybody's advantage. How? Very often, management will push a "down" employee to do better. They will shout encouragement, egg the employee to stay focused, provide sharp training lessons, and hope the agent can stick-it-out. This is not always the right way to manage an agent who is having a poor day. Instead, here is a scenario to explore. The supervisor should acknowledge that the employee is not having a great day and allow the employee to take an extended break, leave for the day, or perform other activities that will benefit the entire call center and the agent. When an employee is 'down", the supervisor may want to encourage him to stop selling for the day or answering the phone, and instead do ride-along monitoring sessions with another agent. The supervisor can even offer to sit on the telephone for his agent, and provide his agent the ability to play "supervisor" for the day. (That would excite many employees!) If the "down" agent is usually a top producer in the department, the supervisor can encourage that employee to use his/her experience and skills to assist an agent who hasn't yet found the same success. Just because an employee is overcome with negative emotions does not mean that the employee is wasted for the day. Nor does it mean the supervisor should force that agent to continue doing their primary job for the day. Instead, that "down" employee can use his talents elsewhere until he is ready to get back on the telephone and excel. I have always believed that a negative agent on the telephone is worth less than having no agent on the telephone at all. The supervisor can respect the agent's negative "down" emotions, while trying to turn them into a positive for him, another agent if applicable, and the entire department. I have even been known to tell call center agents to go home with full pay for the day when they are purely in the dumps. Certainly, I lose production that day, but how much production would I have received from them anyhow? And isn't one person with negative emotions an unattractive distraction to a call center department?

When agents are negative on the call center floor, the supervisor must get them away from the floor into a place where they can channel their negative emotions away from their peers.

Eight times out of ten times, the agent performs better the very next day than they ever would have if the supervisor had made him/her stay in their regular job. The loyalty and admiration the supervisor gains from his employees is limitless. Usually, agents perform better that next day than they would have in the next two days combined had they stayed on the telephone. This form of empathy is a guaranteed way to take an agent's emotions and ensure that those emotions beget success.

Agents see their job as one that doesn't allow much flexibility. Usually their desk is small and their job is to stay put. This doesn't initially express positive emotions to the agents. But, the call center doesn't have to be restrictive if the supervisor is intelligent enough to recognize how agents are motivated to break records. It is naive to believe that emotions don't play a factor in managing call center agents. They play a factor in managing life at home, with friends and family, and with peers at work. Why wouldn't they play a factor in managing call center agents? When someone is emotionally unhappy with something at home, they have the flexibility and ability to go elsewhere; another room, the television, a book, other people, the backyard, etc. Escape works to regain the positive emotions that bring success. Why can't agents have those same opportunities at work? It is the job of the supervisor to be intuitive about emotions and their impact on call center agents.

> In the customer contact center, the noise level should be loud so it encourages *movement* and *expression.*

CHAPTER 7

Understanding, Creating And Initiating Agent Feedback Opportunities

"Having a sense of purpose in your life is the most important element of becoming a fully functioning person."

Wayne Dyer, psychologist and writer

Clearly, agents excel when their feedback becomes a critical piece to developing a powerful, performance-based culture within your call center. Everything in this book will fail if your call center doesn't take the initiative to put communicating and feedback at the forefront of the agent/management philosophy. Fundamentally, asking for and utilizing agent feedback is a concept that most call centers simply don't implement. Call Centers which are stagnant or in a growth spurt alike are painfully inept at building feedback opportunities for agents. The stress for management to meet deadlines and goals gets in the way of creating opportunities for agents to help management meet deadlines and goals. If senior management would take its supervisors in a room and ask them what their job objectives are, supervisors probably would not mention "To create effective channels of agent feedback." Yet, isn't that exactly what supervisors should be doing?

Agents thrive on providing feedback. They need to feel a sense of contribution. The opportunity to air their opinions, by providing feedback to management at all levels, is invaluable to them. Feedback will always exist between agent and supervisor. However, successful feedback is established via the supervisor. Agents wait for supervisors to open up channels so agents can communicate. Let's not forget that the average employee spends far more of their prime/core day at work than anywhere else. We may only spend eight hours at work, but after a 45 minute drive each way, our downtime both physically, emotionally and spiritually is at home. Our primetime is at the office. Therefore, employees want to make their work environment as "home happy" as possible. The following question reveals the facts. If you were not allowed to contribute at home; if your feedback at home was ignored; if your opinions at home weren't encouraged and instituted, wouldn't you want to go somewhere else? The responsibility to create feedback begins with the supervisor.

Even when feedback *is* encouraged, management's skill in proactively acting upon agent feedback is another story. For instance, management may want feedback, but when they get it, they may not utilize it. Perhaps management desires to put together a unit of agents to help create contests for the department. This is a good form of developing agent feedback opportunities. Management may call for volunteers and convene meetings. However, what happens if, after one or two meetings, management begins to focus on other programs or ideas, and lets this idea wither away? Agents lose a sense of belonging. Their hopes, which were so high when the teams were developed, become fears that their position in the company isn't valued. Agents lose confidence in their supervisors to act and implement. This is so common in call centers that I wouldn't doubt if you are experiencing a similar situation right now.

To be successful, agent feedback incorporates a consortium of tenets. Management isn't expected to be exceptional at each. However, management must take the necessary steps to become proficient in as many areas as possible. Some of the most important are as follows:

1. Develop accessible channels for agents to contribute to the call center. Channels may include team meetings, team assignments, mini-group seminars, one-on-one chats, etc.

2. Create specific and spontaneous opportunities for agents to contribute.

3. Encourage agents to contribute to the call center through ask and reward.

4. Encourage agents to contribute to the call center through internal motivation.

5. Utilize agent contributions by implementation and demonstration.

6. Respond to agent feedback utilizing management feedback.

7. Build a feedback culture that focuses on behaviors and values.

8. Use agent feedback opportunities to develop motivation for agents.

9. Turn feedback within the call center into hands-on growth opportunities for agents.

Do you remember the phrase *"Kids should be seen but not heard"?* Management has been known to subscribe to this adage. Some managers believe that agents, front line supervisors and even middle management should be seen but not heard. For instance, executive management has a direction they want to take, and pity anybody who gets in their way. (Anyhow, isn't that what a suggestion box is for?) A common reason why management does a terrible job facilitating agent feedback, of course, is that management is so consumed with putting out fires, meeting objectives and running day-to-day call center operations that they have little time or energy to instigate agent feedback. Some supervisors are exhausted, some are burnt out in their jobs, and some don't know how to make feedback happen. Most can't see the enormous benefits from agent feedback. Others may have the desire, but not the plan. Perhaps management forgets the call center is not only their call center, but their agents' call center, too. Let's be clear: I believe that most managers want constructive feedback that will assist operations and performance. They want all employees to feel empowered to provide constructive feedback. When reminded, they encourage open communication. Only a small fraction of management truly feels compelled to ignore agent feedback. A more important reason why management does a mediocre job facilitating agent feedback is because management does not recognize how to make it happen. Questions such as the following are commonplace:

"Now that we have a few great ideas, how do we make them happen?"

"How do we involve agents in making these great ideas come to fruition?"

"Who has the time to institute these ideas that sound worthwhile?"

"How do we provide feedback to agents about all the feedback we have received?"

Have you ever heard management invite agent feedback using some combination of the following sentences?

"Please make your comments constructive and worthwhile."

"Don't be negative."

"I want proactive, positive feedback."

"You are being negative and complaining, and that won't get us anywhere."

These concepts, delivered by management, troubles me, for two main reasons:

1. *Management wants only feedback from agents that is constructive and worthwhile.* Whose opinion is it that a particular piece of feedback is deemed constructive and worthwhile? The agent's, the supervisor's, the senior manager's? Why wouldn't non-constructive or non- worthwhile feedback still be valuable? Must the agents who provide feedback refrain from communicating because they worry that what they say might be construed by management as not being constructive or worthwhile? What kind of communication culture is management putting in place?

2. *Management wants only feedback that isn't negative. They want proactive and positive feedback. You are being negative and*

complaining, and that won't get us anywhere. In other words, don't tell management anything but what they want to hear? In other words, if your feedback is proactive, truthful, and lends negativity to something or somebody or some policy, withhold it? Management probably has the most fragile egos of any call center employees. They deem negative feedback as something meaningless. They are afraid to take that negative feedback and believe it. But what if what they consider negative feedback is really an agent's attempt to help improve the call center? Is that not really a positive form of feedback? "Don't be negative" is a one-liner management uses all of the time. But when it comes to feedback, asking for feedback with no negativity is like asking for feedback that is filtered of meaning.

Very often, management communicates many of these zingers, either to one another or to their agents. Management thinks they are being "proactive" by setting "ground rules" and keeping "positive spirit". The fact is, management is asking for communication that won't amount to a hill of beans. Results do not occur when management hears only what it chooses to hear. Building strong agent feedback begins with the premise that management must initiate the process and set the parameters. Management must play an active role to accept and facilitate feedback. Management's desire for agents to contribute feedback must be genuine. Management must take the limits off feedback and eliminate the ground rules. If there is one suggestion box in the call center, management must add three more, and figure out ways to bring those suggestion boxes to life. For example, if your call center has e-mail, set up a "suggestion address". If your company has an intranet site, set up a suggestion page.

Building agent feedback within the culture of the call center helps the call center in the following ways:

♦ Feedback incorporates the agent into the flow of the call center.
♦ Agents feel they are an integral part of the organization.
♦ Feedback increases retention.
♦ Feedback builds a phenomenal environment.
♦ Feedback makes the agent feel appreciated.
♦ Feedback helps management in operating the call center by guiding them in the right direction.
♦ Feedback helps management delivers results.
♦ Agent feedback creates a symbiosis between management and agents that lifts the entire communication culture of the call center.

Let's look at some of the ways agent feedback may be delivered to management:

♦ Agent feedback may be requested or offered.
♦ Agent feedback may be formal or informal.
♦ Agent feedback may be written or verbal.
♦ Agent feedback may be consistently produced or inconsistently produced.
♦ Agent feedback may be planned or spontaneous.
♦ Agent feedback may require or not require follow-up.
♦ Agent feedback may arise from planned or impromptu meetings.
♦ Agent feedback may originate from e-mail, letters, notes, or from verbal communication.
♦ Agent feedback may be asked for.
♦ Agent feedback may be conditioned through ongoing practices.
♦ Agent feedback may be orchestrated through standard contests or impromptu games performed on a weekly or monthly basis.

Orchestrating Agent Feedback Through Human Nature

If you took a few moments to identify why some call center managers develop, implement and utilize world famous agent feedback programs, while others fail, you might throw dozens of ideas around. In years of brainstorming, I've always had ideas as to why some managers were simply better than others. It wasn't until a few years back that I took all those ideas and narrowed them down into one simple concept: ***Human Nature***. Managers who understand human nature recognize how to implement agent feedback opportunities. They recognize how to use those opportunities to improve performance. They see the value of agent feedback in the call center.

Call Center management is a seminar on human nature; motivating employees, understanding their emotions, balancing situations between your view and their view, humanity, etc. It also includes dealing with agent issues while keeping that agent, and all that agent's peers, focused. Building a contact center that succeeds involves taking the principles of human nature and understanding their place within the context of your structure. Human Nature involves creating relationships between people; recognizing birthdays, congratulating accomplishments, etc. If your structure celebrates these areas of human nature that are valuable to agents, then agents will respond appropriately. If your call center does not, then human nature will build an appropriate response by agents. Any plan to initiate agent feedback will fail if the agent doesn't see the supervisor as somebody who really wants to make agent feedback work. The supervisor must understand the basic principles of human nature to go beyond knowing his employees. Management must reach out, understand their employees' passion, and in a sense become them. Why are they here? What are their lives like away from work? Where were they before coming here? What makes them tick? Why do they want to provide feedback? What channels would they utilize to provide feedback? Agents can sense very quickly whether a supervisor has a sense for human nature. For instance, the practices of identifying "wants" and "needs" in the world of telesales training transcends to call center management. When management can clearly separate an agent's "want" desire from an agent's "need" desire, the manager has become a world class leader. I teach in sales training workshops that clients either "want" or "need" a product or service, but rarely do they both "want" *and* "need" a product or service. A "want" is a very emotional desire. Examples include wanting ice cream; wanting a new home; and wanting to ditch school for the wrong reasons because it feels good to do so. A "need" is very logical and practical. Examples include needing to eat a healthy dinner; needing to purchase the most cost-affordable home; and needing to miss school for the right reason because it makes sense to do so. Human nature is dictated by "wants" and "needs".

> Ask your agents questions. Get them talking. Find out about them. Get them to talk about their thoughts and needs. Have them answer your questions.

So is the nature of call center agents. When an agent demands attention, a supervisor must identify whether that agent "needs" special attention, or merely "wants" attention. Through questions and experience, a supervisor can learn from the agents where their desires stand. Perhaps with agent W, every issue is a "need", and involves special attention. A quick meeting with agent W will automatically involve a one hour stop-over. Therefore, the supervisor plans. Based on this identification, the supervisor may conclude how much time can be spent with every agent based upon crisis and conversation. A key facet of feedback is simple — identify each of your agents, their "needs" and their "wants".

For example, group discussions are a study of human nature. I am a big fan of group discussions in the call center. Sometimes management shies away from group discussions because they feel they might get "pounded" by their agents; a kind of "rant and rave" session. However, group discussions allow management to hear multiple opinions, and they give agents an opportunity to bounce their opinions off their peers. A group discussion can open windows of opportunity for both agents and management. For instance, each time management comes away "pounded" from a group discussion whether they heard negative feedback or not, they can be assured that the concepts and passions behind those comments existed long before they were spoken. Human nature exists whether or not management believes in it or chooses to accept it. Therefore, isn't it better to know what is behind the façade? Most group discussions don't become "gripe sessions" if managed properly. A foundation for these meetings must be established. For example, below are listed the issues that management must resolve prior to implementing group discussions:

Why is management holding a group discussion in the first place?
What major objectives may be reached as a result of the discussions?
Is the meeting planned on a regular basis or is it impromptu?
Are agents selected based on qualifications, or selected randomly?
Who is moderating the discussion?
Are the topics pre-planned or impromptu?
When will management hold another group discussion?
Does management intend on meeting with every agent or a selection of agents?
Is agent feedback the number one priority of these meetings?
How will feedback be handled once received?
Where will these meetings take place?

Bringing a group of three to ten agents into a room and chatting is a simple way to create agent feedback. The first few meetings may be awkward, as both sides try to decide what they want to accomplish. Once agents see that group discussions are a regular aspect of the communication culture, the group discussions regularly become an opportunity forum.

Here are two group meeting scenarios you may want to review. A senior level manager meets with all agents one time each month. This is a fantastic opportunity for that manager to ask questions and receive feedback. If the meetings were held only once a year, feedback would be stifled; ground rules would be fragmented; confidence amongst agents would be nil. But because meetings are consistent and frequent, a foundation is in place. At every meeting, the senior manager communicates a fifteen to twenty minute presentation, and he encourages questions along the way. Once completed, he asks for, and receives, dialogue. Agents become comfortable with the routine, and past experiences in this setting reaffirm to them that their questions, comments and feedback will be listened to and addressed with respect.

In another scenario, the situation is completely reversed. A senior level manager speaks only once a year. Agent feedback is non-existent. The manager continues to grope for feedback, but the agents are stone silent. Why? Because there is no sense of relationship between the two parties. There is no sense of structure or foundation to the presentation. Agents don't feel confident about expressing feedback. Nobody wants to be coddled and encouraged and persuaded to provide feedback, only to be ignored, or ridiculed.

Agent feedback is limited. The audience clams up because they are unsure of the reaction with which their comments will be met.

In both these scenarios, agent feedback was asked for, considered, and in one fashion or another, received. But note how human nature played a role in feedback. Agents felt comfortable in the first meeting because they knew the parameters. They had no comfort level in the second meeting, because the parameters were unknown. Agents need to be provided with consistency and opportunity in order for feedback to work. They need to know that a meeting with a senior executive will not be their only meeting. If agents believe they have a one-shot deal when they are called into a room, little will get accomplished. I have been part of a management team that decided to meet with selected call center agents. I asked why. The answer given was so they could hear what was happening "on the floor". There was a desire to receive agent feedback. I asked if we had any set agenda. The answer was no. I made it clear to the management team that this was okay. However, I wanted to emphasize that we, as a management team, would get back from our agents what we put into this. They would give us agent feedback based on the parameters we set. It was our ballgame.

Agent Characteristics

Management must base agent feedback on the characteristics of the agents in the call center. Good managers recognize human nature. They can see under which circumstances certain agents will open up and communicate. They can also visualize other circumstances wherein the more reluctant agents will participate. Through this recognition, management can build feedback opportunities to meet the needs of every class of agents. Those agents who beg to provide feedback don't always have the most to say. Those not interested in management communication may have plenty to contribute. The opportunity to provide feedback and the expected quality of feedback should not be determined by the willingness to provide feedback. Some of the great idea makers and suggestions in a call center come from agents who seem oblivious to the importance of providing feedback to management. Most call centers have a mix of agents. For instance, some beg to talk with management, just to be seen. They have little to contribute. They may feel lonely, or ignored, and they want to communicate so they can get in front of management as often as possible. Imagine a feedback room with these "needy" agents, each one fighting for attention. How much feedback can be received and analyzed? How constructive would a meeting like this be? On the other hand, some agents only want to communicate when extremely motivated to do so. You probably have a few call center agents who stay quiet and to themselves until given an opportunity to provide feedback. Would a group of introverted, shy agents provide a successful group discussion? Should feedback be initiated with agents who don't appear to want to provide feedback? Is a mixture desired? To help answer these questions, remember that agent characteristics generally fall into one of these five categories, which I call the five P's:

1. Possession
2. Prominence
3. Peer Pressure
4. Personal Improvement
5. Personal (Family) Life

By identifying these categories as they relate to each agent, management will be more successful in developing feedback opportunities. Those agents who want to feel like they can be accountable for what happens in the work environment fall into the possession mode. Those agents who feel that consistent communications will move them to the head of the class, in terms of opportunity and respect, fall into the prominence mode. Those agents who provide feedback to their supervisors oftentimes do so because of peer pressure. For example, perhaps other agents are happy with something going on in the call center and the agent who comes to you wants to communicate why he feels he should be a part of the action, or maybe his peers have motivated the agent in some way to come forth and talk to the supervisors. Personal Improvement is the number one reason agents want to communicate feedback. They communicate to benefit their own standings. Finally, when the goal is to benefit their own standings, what agents really are doing is looking out for their personal (Family) life. One part of this family they are looking at is their extended family, the call center family. The second family agents acknowledge is their family at home. Simply put, most of us work to support our life away from work. It would be great if we worked two days a week and enjoyed our personal life for five days a week. In most industries, that just doesn't happen.

When management acknowledges these agent characteristics, they begin the process of creating a communication culture which favors feedback, and a greater understanding of where the agents are coming from. If, for instance, some agents are taking long lunches or breaks, and an agent who is not doing this comes to you, it is pretty clear that the agent feels his peers have an unfair opportunity in the world of personal improvement. If an agent comes to you to complain about commission plans, salary structures, data campaigns, talk time percentages or any other call center issues, the primary reason they are doing it is likely for personal improvement.

CHAPTER 8

Communicating Through Channels And Messages

"To a man with an empty stomach, food is God"　　　　*Gandhi*

The great challenge for any supervisor in a leadership role is to motivate the individual, and the whole, successfully. The call center world is one that truly encompasses both the individual and the whole. While the supervisor sees his entire unit as one entity that needs motivation, passion, instruction and guidance, he must also recognize each agent as an individual apart from the group. Have you noted how a basketball coach can successfully influence the entire team at one stage, while successfully influencing individual team members at another? Phil Jackson, a seven time world championship coach, is renowned for being able to communicate to both the team and the individual for maximum effect. Prior to long road trips and before seasons begin, he is legendary for giving each player a book specific to him so he can read that book, and glean insights on a particular topic. As the team travels from city to city throughout a long season, Jackson builds learning blocks based on each player. As a whole unit, he is communicating one message by asking each player to read a book and learn from it. Each player takes away something from this general statement. However, Jackson is also tailoring each book and each message specifically to each player, thereby communicating an individual message as well. Other athletic coaches, such as John Wooden (10 national championships) and Mike Krzyzewski (two titles in the 1990's) also have methods of motivating the entire unit while keeping each player focused on individual responsibility. Jackson, Wooden and Mike Krzyzewski are some of the few coaches who have mastered the objective of communicating to the whole and individual in a way that meets objectives and produces results. Their communication is effective.

Management can tailor messages for maximum effectiveness. Communicating begins with coordinating the message. For example, political candidates are coached to stay on message. They are told not to drift from one message to another, because the intended recipients will get confused. Most importantly, political candidates lend different styles to the same message, based upon the audience. A political candidate may speak about cultural issues first to a small group and then to a large group, and communicate the same message differently. Depending on dozens of factors, political candidates use the same general message, and separate styles of delivering that message in order to impress each individual on his own level. A group may hear a stump speech whereas an individual may receive a warm comment or two. Both styles are meant to deliver the same message and to meet a common objective.

What messages must be sent? How do you want to send them? I have found that agents are often so consumed with their jobs that they find it difficult to understand the intent of group communication. The supervisor must simplify the messages *and aim them directly at the* intended recipients. In many instances, communication in a group setting is a difficult venue in which to ensure the agent understands. How often have you seen a manager articulate a simple concept to a group, only to have the group scratching their heads in confusion after the meeting? In a group setting, agents tend to ignore what they consider to be peripheral and focus on the messages they want to hear. Depending on the situation, those messages may be positive or negative. Unfortunately, the parts they ignore may be more valuable than the aspects they remember. In some instances, managers who conduct group meetings recognize right away that a large percentage of the communication they articulated was misplaced. The next day, they say "Hey, I told them in the meeting about the benefits change, but nobody heard it because they were disappointed over the price increase."

Speaking for the purpose of creating noise will get nothing accomplished. The supervisor must commit to accomplishing some simple goals. Supervisors must remember that a call center agent's daily job is to talk with people via the telephone, and receive and communicate messages in that fashion. They don't desire to hear a supervisor provide chatter without the messages laid out simply. For example, if they are customer service agents, they probably hear chatter without message all of the time from their prospects and have learned to gloss over much of it. Team meetings each day are perfect examples of chatter with no goals. Agents don't need to hear chatter with no goals — they get enough of that on the telephone.

In **Friendly Persuasion**, my book on telesales training, I state as follows:

"When a pedestrian hears warning bells at a railroad crossing, he acts and reacts. When someone in an argument hears statements by the other party, he also acts and reacts. In our society, often we attempt to communicate but we don't accummulate information or assimilate it. For example, we may hear a report on a news or talk radio station (or at least we think we're hearing it!), and then not remember anything the newscaster or radio personality said two

minutes later. (i.e. Did the sportscaster say our team won the game? Did the woman in the helicopter say there was an accident on this freeway or on another one?) We might sit at the dinner table for two hours and talk with a group of people, only to come away with no understanding of or gain from the conversation. In some ways, society has conditioned us not to relate.

TSRs, as members of our society, are subject to the above-described weaknesses. When on the telephone, TSRs fight this conditioning every time they make a presentation. The TSR's ability to truly listen and hear becomes most crucial when one realizes that a TSR's success or failure at work depends on his mastery of these skills."

Communicating to individual agents involves conditioning agents to comprehend central messages. Agents respond based on past conditioning. Agents respond to the way you talk to them based on how they wish you would talk to them. Agents learn how individual conversations have unfolded in the past, and they build on this knowledge. For instance, each time supervisors talk about meeting goals for the week, agents have learned through past conversations whether or not this communication is meaningful. If the same topic has come up in the past, were there any consequences? For example, if the supervisor discussed in the past the fact that agents were not answering the telephone fast enough, but there was no penalty for it, why would those same agents feel that any penalty would ensure if the supervisor communicated this time that they were not picking up inbound calls fast enough? Or, if every time the manager holds his clip-board on the main sales floor it means his agents must be cognizant of their team's production for the day, why does this communication from supervisor to agent matter if supervisors don't reward or penalize agents based on production?

Supervisors should recognize that words, comments and expressions are taken less seriously when presented in a group setting. For example, in the restaurant business, the manager may have a shift meeting with his staff of twenty and explain that tables need to be turned over faster than they presently are. Clearly, this is a general statement that tables are not being turned over fast enough. It is not a reflection on every waiter and waitress, because a certain percentage of those waiters and waitresses are turning over their tables fast enough. The message has been sent in group fashion, and each person reviews it subjectively. If the supervisor then takes the time to go to each person and provide additional follow-up on that topic, the group communication becomes the foundation for the message, not the message itself.

Perhaps in your call center a supervisor may communicate that talk time is up, and agents are spending too long with each customer. Therefore, the message is that agents need to get their talk time down. Clearly, not every agent has this problem, but the message the supervisor sends is being articulated to the entire group. How effective will this message be if the supervisor also articulates three other messages, and then spends ten minutes articulating four new messages? Initial topics become forgotten while only messages specifically designed for agents become valued. If, for instance, a supervisor encourages his team of agents to perform better because the group is not meeting performance goals, the supervisor must understand that not all the agents truly need to perform better. Many are already performing at acceptable levels. The supervisor must realize that of those agents performing at acceptable levels, a large segment are taken aback at the fact that the message is even relayed to them. If not handled well, the group for which the message isn't intended may take offense. I very often preface some of my statements in a team meeting with the comment "This doesn't apply to everyone, and if this doesn't apply to you then I'd like you to just listen and understand I am directing this to those it does apply to…"

Instruments That Enable Communication To Agents In Both Group And Individual Settings

One way to effectively introduce communication within the call center is through the use of voice mail. We touched upon voice mail earlier in the book, but here is the skinny on voice mail: It is a truly amazing instrument of communication. Once or twice a week, when I want to motivate both team and individuals, I send a "global" voice mail to the entire group, and I follow that up with specific vignettes to four or five agents. It is valuable to note that this system works perfectly when the agent hears the "global" voice mail message first followed by the personal voice mail message. By doing this, I connect to the agent on two levels. When sending the widely distributed voice mail, I impart a specific message to each agent. When sending the personal message to a select few, I comment on specific themes I feel will benefit them.

Good voice mail message have a trick to them. The supervisor must communicate a central message, followed by just a few minor messages to support the central story. For instance, when supervisors leave lengthy messages, agents tend to delete them before the supervisor is finished. Therefore, when I make the error of leaving a rambling voice mail, I throw a trinket on the end. Trinkets such as "If you are still listening, come to my office and I'll buy you a donut and coffee this morning" work exceptionally well. One should see the reaction on the floor. In addition, when a supervisor leaves many voice mail messages, agents have a tendency not to be motivated by them. Hence, one voice mail is the same as the next voice mail, and they mean nothing. The voice mail communication approach becomes repetitive and diluted.

The personal voice mail is quite different, however. As long as the supervisor has something motivational and useful to communicate, agents feel a bond strengthen when they receive personal voice mail from their supervisor. Personal voice mail is a great way to accentuate individual communication.

Another strong communication tool is the utilization of personal notes. I have found personal notes to be the most effective form of one-on-one communication. Every week, I choose a certain percentage of the staff to write notes to. I leave the notes on their chairs, on their desks, in their mail slots, by their telephones or taped to their computers. The verbiage isn't particularly grand. It focuses on one or two concepts I want to communicate to the agent. I may say "Great job yesterday" or "Nice going on a few calls I heard" or "I just wanted to remind you how much we value your professional work ethic". No matter what the note says, it is designed to convey something unexpected that will boost the agent's outlook. Needless to say, this short note which might take forty-five seconds to write becomes a valuable piece of individual communication that pays off extreme dividends for the supervisor. Don't be surprised to see your notes taped up on the agents' side of the wall where everyone can see them!

Another great form of communication is e-mail. E-mail is a fun and dynamic tool that can benefit call center management when used well. Today and in the future, many if not all call centers will have e-mail to use, but prior to the mid-1990's, only a few centers had e-mail, and even fewer used it well. The value of e-mail is that agents don't need to take time off the telephone to check it as they do with voice mail. Agents can easily be talking on the telephone and checking their e-mail at the same time, thereby continuing their primary job functions. E-mail works quite the same way as personal notes, but its impact is less personal.

Recognition and appreciation are the number one job considerations that motivate employees most. E-mail, voice mail and note writing effectively communicate recognition and appreciation to the agent in ways that no other channels of communication can. For instance, a short e-mail delivered to an agent who has no expectations that the e-mail is coming can "make his day". An e-mail that includes sales training or product communication can benefit the agent during or after a call. Creative communication on the call center floor can achieve results in your call center.

. . . .

"Service to others is the rent you pay for your room here on earth."
Muhammad Ali

When management takes steps to ensure that agents feel a special relationship, agents tend to go that extra mile to ensure that they exceed goals. A supervisor's job is to have thirty different relationships with thirty different agents, while allowing each one of those agents to believe there is something special about their particular relationship. Supervisors who accomplish this goal are supervisors who productively create feedback opportunities in the call center.

Management must recognize its unique role in the supervisor /agent connection. First, many non-call center departments can never establish the type of relationship a call center supervisor and agent can establish. Supervisors need to build on this when they communicate with agents. Do agents understand the special relationship that exists only in a call center? Probably not. Supervisors can share that with them, and create a bond. Other supervisors may not see their employees for days or weeks at a time. Call Center supervisors see their agents all of the time. Other supervisors may not be required to motivate and coach their employees in the ways that call center supervisors must. If the call center shift is four hours in length, the supervisor and his agents mingle for all of those four hours. There is little downtime. Supervisors and agents interact constantly. Human Nature, and human emotions, become tested. This also forms the basis for a solid relationship.

Yet supervisors often fail to see how that close relationship can blossom into a foundation which increases department performance. Again, we can focus on how the "human nature" element of the job affects feedback. I like to tell supervisor applicants that any person can supervise a variety of basic jobs if they choose to do so. If a supervisor applicant wants a role supervising those employees picking vegetables or filing claims or typing news releases or punching numbers, that can take place in any one of a million departments throughout the world. Yet supervisor applicants that demonstrate a passion for their job and their agents are very difficult to find, and harder to develop. If applicants can sell me on passion, they can sell it to their agents. That is their job. Passion about their job, and for their agents, is a philosophy that the best call center managers understand. With passion, management relishes the opportunities to involve themselves in solving their agents' issues *prior* to their becoming issues. Management uses passion to involve themselves in creating ways to make the call center and its culture even better than it already is. A supervisor is responsible for staging the environment. A supervisor's objective is to get his agents to say:

> *"The reason you get the most out of your employees is
> because your employees know they don't need to worry
> about what you are thinking. We recognize we can take a break and not*

*suffer a penalty for it. We also recognize we can work extra
hard to make up for the extra break we
took. You provide us with the independence to be adults,
and you don't treat us like elementary school children.
It makes a difference."*

Agents have worked for some terrible bosses in their time. A terrible boss gets that title from a subjective employee. However, any agent can easily describe in simple detail the difference between a good boss and a terrible boss. A good boss has passion, and a bad boss lacks it. A good boss consistently applies introspection to his job. A bad boss doesn't want to be troubled. A good boss works hard at creating a special relationship of communication and culture with each agent. A poor boss doesn't have time.

In addition, management does understand some tenets of call center supervision. Management recognizes that agents don't leave their jobs for "greener pastures" when they feel they are respected. We recognize that agents don't leave when they feel they are making good money, and when they are making good money for the work they do. We recognize that agents don't leave when they like their environment. But do we realize that agents don't leave because you say "good morning" to them every day? As silly as it may sound, agents thrive on being touched emotionally no matter how superficially, by their supervisor. I always counsel that no matter how many agents you have, it is mandatory that you spend from ten seconds to two minutes with each one every single day. Saying "good morning" each day builds a special relationship between supervisor and agent that 90% of all supervisors around the country do not foster. If you emotionally touch each person consistently, you announce to each agent how special and important that person is to the success of the company. You build a fantastic relationship.

When I managed a staff of 250 agents, I knew I couldn't go around the room and talk to each one of them every day. I also had managers and supervisors who were required to do that with their team members, so I knew the personal touch was being provided. It wasn't enough for me. I wanted to do something with my agents that let them know that everyone in the call center cared. Therefore, I made it a point of being at the entrance, and exit, every day. When people arrived to work, I was there to greet them. For fifteen minutes, I talked one-by-one with each agent as they walked through the door. Then again, at closing time, I was at the door again, providing words of encouragement and a positive slap on the back as they walked through the door to go home. On my part, it wasn't easy. I had to schedule meetings around those times, and I had to make sure I wasn't busy doing something else when those times arrived. In the process, of course, I learned the most valuable lesson of all. 90% of all the other call center directors in the world do not do that. Agents know! In addition, I accomplished a variety of other objectives by simply making the second effort.

1. Retention improved.
2. Performance improved.
3. Culture improved.
4. Feedback from agents to management improved.
5. Solutions to problems became very proactive.
6. I accomplished much more on the floor with agents in five second bursts than I ever could have accomplished otherwise.
7. A relationship developed between the agents, myself, and my staff that encouraged agent feedback.

Because agents talk constantly on the telephone, we sometimes forget that they miss the little interactions with human beings that they don't find in their daily routine on the telephone. Therefore, the objective is to find opportunities to build a relationship that stands out. Taking agents to lunch, inviting them to the movies during work hours, taking them off the telephones for snacks and letting them go home early are four key ways to play the trust game. Many call center supervisors don't do these four things because they feel it would be unlike a supervisor to ask agents to lunch, invite them to movies during work hours, give them free food, or let them leave early from work. The opposite is true.

In call centers with an inbound focus, managers are overly concerned with service level functions and answering the telephones properly. This mindset has been ingrained in supervisors by their bosses, who had it ingrained by their bosses. Keeping agents on the telephone meets objectives. Although keeping customers holding on the telephone so a supervisor may eat ice cream with a few agents is not the way to run a business, I believe that is an extreme example of the interaction that makes world class call centers succeed. One concept managers need to keep in mind is "Don't manage harder - manage smarter." Agents realize that they need to be on the telephone to answer calls. They understand numbers. Hence, when a supervisor asks one or two agents to get off the telephone and join him for ice cream at the very time when the phones are busiest and the agents are most stressed, the supervisor is telling his agents that something is of even greater importance to him than calls. Them! This message sings volumes, and, in actuality, the message doesn't have to be so dramatic. For example, agents in downtime with little call volume would probably relish the opportunity to eat ice cream in a feedback and communication session with their supervisor. In a down period, when agents are bored and willing to do anything other than talk on the telephone to another stranger, it is the perfect opportunity for the supervisor to bring several agents into the break room, or down the street, for a snack. Action is paramount. Most supervisors do not exploit downtime to their advantage. They know the telephones aren't ringing, but they don't act. Or they use that time for themselves. All the while, they miss a great opportunity to help themselves as well as their agents, on a long term basis.

Below are some of the key areas of agent supervision that supervisors must be aware of. The goal for supervisors is to place each of these areas within the context of their own operations. Although the differences between supervising telesales and customer service agents are extremely slim, some aspects, such as being late to work, may be more of a priority when managing inbound customer service agents than outbound telesales agents. Still, telesales and customer service agents both are required to show up on time and meet minimum standards on the telephone. Supervisors must be cognizant with regard to their shifts. In the case of telesales agents, it may be more important that agents meet their minimum sales numbers. Whereas in the case of customer service agents, it may be more valuable that they arrive promptly to work so customers may have their telephone calls answered properly. Senior management needs to determine exactly what they want their supervisors to monitor, and how strict they want that monitoring to be.

Key Areas of Agent Supervision

1. Being late to work.
2. Coming late from break.
3. Failing to move to the next call or e-mail after one is completed.
4. Coming back late from lunch.
5. Incorrectly handling a customer/prospect issue.
6. Setting poorly qualified appointments or sales.
7. Leaving work early.
8. Communicating on the telephone poorly.
9. Staying off the telephone for too long.
10. Spending too much time working on personal projects.
11. Being rude on the telephone.
12. Being insubordinate to a supervisor.
13. Treating teammates and peers inadequately.
14. Failing to meet goals and objectives.
15. Not adapting to changes within the call center.

. . . .

"Knowing your own darkness is the best method for dealing with the darkness of other people." Carl Jung

Supervisors who do good things for their agents and still receive negative feedback find their day-to-day job to be irritating. I have never enjoyed supervising agents who didn't believe I was giving my all for them. Primarily, I have to feel this stems from the fact that I actually care too much about my work, and I let my personal emotions get in the way of my job successes. (I call this the Mr. Spock supervisor battle, because Spock always cared about his work, and battled his personal emotions in the workplace.) For instance, I once invited five agents to go to lunch with me. Four declined. Why? Because the four-star restaurant I was willing to spend my own money at wasn't good enough for them — they wanted better! From my management perspective, it became extremely difficult to become motivated to help these people excel. When a supervisor does quality work, perhaps by going out of his way to make an agent's job easier or more productive, the supervisor is doing the right things. When the supervisor hears grapevine feedback that agents are unhappy with the way that he has performed, the supervisor has the right to be upset. "What in the world do they want!" "What more can I do!" Supervisors run into this problem all of the time. In fact, some supervisors never know what their agents say about them, because they aren't in touch with what is going on away from the call center. That type of supervisor rolls straight ahead without being touched, because the glancing blows dealt him are never received. Other supervisors run into the dilemma of overhearing what their agents say about them, thereby creating bad will, or disappointment, between agent and supervisor. Great supervisors brush this off as a natural part of communication, as we'll discuss in a moment. Other supervisors become ego-whipped. For example, one supervisor I mentored went to lunch and stood behind a wall, listening to four of his agents attacking his sales abilities and telesales experience for five minutes. Listening to this really hurt him! He could feel his sense of accomplishment dwindle. He was also exasperated, because he had spent countless hours working hard to gain the respect and trust of those very agents who were verbally attacking him.

What to do? First, whether the supervisor was standing behind the wall listening to those comments or not, the comments rang true for those speaking them. They probably had been spoken before that time, as well, and will unquestionably be spoken in the future. All a supervisor can do in a case like that is accept the fact that human nature dictates that people will deal blows at their immediate bosses from time to time. It is a part of supervision. As long as the supervisor is confident that his management style, efforts and the decisions he implements are the ones that get results, earn respect, build consistency and achieve success, then the supervisor can do nothing more than forge ahead, even if the agents disagree with his management style and decisions. In other words, the supervisor should expect that his group of agents will be unhappy with him with regard to many issues, and the supervisor should understand that he is also receiving grief that arises from issues away from the call center. He simply needs to chalk this up to human nature, and move forward.

For instance, a majority of the communication about a supervisor in the call center happens at off-times, away from the call center floor. This *gathering of blab*, as I call it, is natural in any work environment, especially those environments that involve quite a few decisions, and quite a few people. Agents talk while on break, while eating lunch, while spending time together after work. Supervisors must recognize this dynamic. Agents comment on the positives and negatives of a supervisor, and they find much more consensus and interest in talking about what could have been done, in their views, as opposed to what was done. Therefore, the supervisor must understand

Supervisors must be comfortable with their relationship to their employees. They are not friends, and can expect their agents to not like many of their decisions.

that addressing the problem is not usually the answer. Suppose a call center agent sets up a meeting with his supervisor, and the agent explains to the supervisor in the context of the work day exactly why the agent is unhappy with the supervisor's work performance. When this happens, it should be addressed and, if necessary, the supervisor should take steps to make changes and provide improvement. Perhaps the agent is right! Perhaps the supervisor can do better than he presently is doing. However, when communication negative to the supervisor is received by the supervisor in non-work related venues, (i.e. *gathering of blab*) then it is extremely important that the supervisor take a step back, reassess what he's heard, recognize the validity if applicable, and move forward in his own ways. Addressing blind issues is not the right way to go about management. If issues aren't directly taken to management, issues should not be directly addressed.

Any supervisor who puts the goal of being liked ahead of any other goal is a supervisor who will eventually be disappointed. Supervisors who put "being liked" first more often would address *gathering of blab* sessions than would those who don't. When I teach supervisors, I teach recognition. "Recognize you are not friends with those who work for you, and recognize you can't make every decision to please everybody. Recognize your objective, which is to build and sustain respect from the agents so the department and business grows and retains performance. Don't feel that you can get them to like you, and don't feel that they can get you to like them. Both parties will only walk away disappointed. Recognize how strong emotions are and the role emotions play within the call center."

Here is another example. I received some startling news seven weeks after starting a call center management job. A new agent who had started just four weeks after me came to me for a private conference and explained that I was vilified every which way in the lunch room by the same clique of seven or eight agents. He was concerned that I wouldn't survive in my job, and he was providing me with some feedback. I listened intently and thanked the agent for passing on the news to me. I also told the agent that nothing said about me away from the call center floor surprised me in the least or concerned me in the least. This, of course, surprised him. Here is a paraphrase of what I told the agent:

"I'm new, and the agents have experience on me in this call center, so they feel they have the upper hand in knowing what is right. Therefore, they will attack. But nothing substantial was ever built overnight, and for me to succeed long term I need to persevere with my program and watch the pieces fall into place. Most likely, in six months the whole call center will look different, feel different, and thrive differently. And those agents attacking me today will still attack me, perhaps a bit lighter, tomorrow. But in the call center six months from now, those agents will succeed and relish the positive performance programs I've put into place, and they will respect the fact that my staff and I are helping them to break records. They may not like me, but they will respect me. The bottom line is that everything the agents are saying today is everything every agent in every call center in every city says about new managers. I would be alarmed if they didn't feel this way. If they didn't feel this way, then I actually would believe I'm not doing the job I've been hired to do. If we told my boss what those agents are saying about me, he would most probably say 'Great Dan, you're doing perfect'. Therefore, let them continue to communicate. I encourage you to watch the nature and tone of their communications change as the weeks and months go by."

I didn't always feel that way. I can still reflect on times when agents I thought I had quality relationships with communicated their disappointment with me to their peers, and sometimes, to my peers. Over time, I began to understand the relationship between supervisor and agent in the call center, and I incorporated a new type of supervisory style. Agents will never be my friends. They will be my employees. I should expect that not all their comments about me will be perfectly complimentary or perfectly negative. They will be mixed based on emotions and events. Coincidentally, my comments about my agents will never be perfectly complimentary, nor will they be completely negative. They will be mixed.

Not every agent will appreciate your leadership. All you can do is remain confident in your skills and abilities. Below are some avenues call center supervisors should consider when it comes to dealing with agents who are unhappy with their leadership.

1. Maintain your inner passion and concentration when agents go on the attack.
2. Remember the role that human nature plays in call center operations.
3. Hear intently what the agents are saying. Look for truths.
4. If applicable, attempt to make changes in your management style.
5. Ignore the *gathering of blab.*

. . . .

He who asks is a fool for five minutes, but he who does
not ask remains a fool forever.
Chinese proverb

Perhaps the most frustrating job for call center management is to face the reality of motivating the agent who is completely de-motivated. This is especially frustrating when that agent has demonstrated himself to be a senior agent, and one of the most productive members of the department.

Veteran agents are the core of any call center. Sales statistics show that 20% of all agents can make as many as 80% of all sales! Veteran agents who are comfortable in their work environment set the foundation for new, or struggling, peers. More than just being top agents, they represent the backbone and possibilities of an entire call center. New Hires look to veterans for history and leadership. Management relies on veterans to help in the daily running of the call center. Veteran Agents are truly the core of an operation.

A challenge call center managers face all of the time is keeping their top agents productive when their top agents choose not to be. The skills of Listening and Hearing are critical, particularly the skill set of hearing. I spent the first section of my telesales book, **Friendly Persuasion,** talking about the value of successfully listening and hearing over the telephone. When it comes to telephone communication, listening and hearing are invaluable. They give the customer trust and confidence. Customers believe, and rightly so, that what they say is heard. Listening and Hearing encapsulates the art of "Friendly Persuasion". Listening and Hearing work when supervising agents as well. In fact, great supervisors listen and hear exceptionally well while doing little talking. The call center supervisor who recognizes the importance of spending time listening to and hearing agents will be the supervisor who helps agents to succeed more often than not.

Listening occurs when the communicator uses verbal nods to encourage the party on the other end to continue speaking. Managers must make agents feel they are being listened to. Hearing, which is the topic we will explore here, incorporates conceptualizing what is being said, so it can be mastered, analyzed and addressed to the call center agent's satisfaction.

Listening and Hearing very much apply to successfully motivating call center agents. We, as management, should always attempt to listen to our agents through verbal and visual nods, such as "uh huh", "keep going" and "I understand." All the while, supervisors must use visual eye contact, note-taking and facial expressions to accentuate the point. I think good supervisors recognize they should always try to listen, although sometimes they may not do it very well. Do you?

Hearing the agent involves understanding the agent. Even when the supervisor believes he understands the agent, he all too often doesn't demonstrate it, through words or actions. Hearing the agent, as we said a few paragraphs ago, involves conceptualizing what the agent means in order to better assist the agent in succeeding. For example, when the agent states that he "will never last through the month and is thinking of changing jobs", he is actually saying "I am struggling and can you please show me how to get out of it. I won't leave here, it's been a good place". When agents leave jobs, they don't give warning. When agents insist they might leave a job, they are crying out for guidance.

Hearing what agents really are saying is critical for a supervisor. I, distressingly, have worked with far too many managers and supervisors who don't make it a point of learning the steps of hearing their agents when their agents communicate. It can be frustrating for all involved.

Take an example of a top agent who is de-motivated. She has been at the company for over two years, and that's veteran status in this department. She has performed far above average each month, meeting goals and maintaining acceptable performance standards.

Then, the collapse. She comes to your office, requests a closed door meeting, and grimaces. She asks for some time without interruption. She whines about all the problems at home and work that have bothered her for quite some time. She is troubled. And this is your core agent! Your bread and butter! This agent is Magic Johnson, Roger Clemens and John Elway all rolled into one. And she is collapsing right in front of you.

This scenario happens quite a bit in call centers. It has probably happened in yours, to you. How do we address it?

Many supervisors take every concern seriously, and while they should take the situation seriously, they should also recognize, through the practice of superior hearing skills, that the issues may be understood and combated in a few simple ways. Here are the steps supervisors should take when meeting with veteran agents in need of counseling.

1. Supervisors should address their top agent's concerns by asking why the issues have come to the forefront now. It's not proper to try to address the issues without first gaining background information. First, the supervisor needs to question the agent on timing. Not only does this draw the agent out of the box of despair, but it allows the supervisor to use hearing skills to understand why the issues are a problem. *Timing is the single most common reason why agents feel compelled to lose their motivation.* When we recognize this, we can use it to our advantage. New agents on their first day on the job rarely lose motivation and need to meet with the manager. Agents who find success at the job in the initial stages of employment (first three months) never ask for a closed door meeting to complain. Veteran agents who experience a resurgence of success are almost never the agents who come to their supervisor for counseling. Hence, timing dictates attitude and motivation. And when dealing with an agent in need of assistance, the timing of the episode needs to be explored.

"What has changed today compared to the past three months, nine months, two years?"

"Is there somebody who has triggered your issues?"

"Are your issues professionally based, personally based, or a combination of the two?"

2. The supervisor should ask the top agent how she would want the situation to be rectified if given an opportunity. This is a simple step many supervisors don't initiate. For some odd reason, supervisors feel they must know answers without asking their agents for guidance, simply because the supervisor is in a supervisory role, and the agent is in a subordinate role. Of course, that's nonsense. Why guess at a solution to a problem when the supervisor can ask the top agent who has the problem for help on a solution? Agents sometimes want to communicate problems, not for resolutions to take place, but to be heard. Nothing wrong with that. What if the supervisor misinterprets the communication and actually makes changes, thinking he is making the correct move? Not good. Supervisors should take notes, hear carefully what is being said, and analyze the communication.

Then, after a pause, the supervisor should say something along the path of the following:

"If you could make some changes- as it sounds like you want me to — what would you do? Give me some solutions."

"I want to help you because I feel I understand what you want. Give me some suggestions."

"If I do X, Y and Z, would you be pleased with that?"

3. The supervisor should ensure he is focused on needs and not on solving an agent's want. It is critical to recognize that the "want" is an emotional experience, and emotions very often dominate the rational mind. If a veteran agent rarely needs assistance but then calls a closed door meeting for help, it can be assumed that emotions have taken control of the situation. That's fine. But providing solutions to an emotional request is only appeasing an employee's "want" cycle. It's a short term response. A limited response. A quick fix. Once the agent's emotional outburst ends, your solutions have lost their validity. Why? Because your solutions solved the "want", and the "want" no longer exists. For instance, I had an agent who came in and complained that he wanted to change seats because he didn't get along with the person across from him. Week after week he would complain about wanting to move, and I would assure him I was looking into the situation but was helpless to move him at the moment, for various reasons. Finally I came to him after two weeks of silence and explained that I had put in an order to move his seat and it had been accepted. His response? "I don't want to move now. We're friends again. Thanks for hearing me out."

4. The supervisor should attempt to discover what the agent needs from the conversation, and attack the needs base. As we discovered, when an agent "wants" action to take place, it's emotional. Any resolution may not achieve the desired objective. However, when an agent "needs" action to take place, the manager can assume the request is logical and legitimate. A "need" is powerful because it implies that without a solution, progress is impossible. For example, if the cause of this problem is that the agent dislikes the person she is sitting across from and "wants" to move, the manager must recognize this dislike for the person may be temporary. If the agent complains that she wants to move because sitting across from that person is stagnating her performance, the manager must analyze through accentuated hearing skills whether a change is in order. One question to consider: If the agent performed well over XYZ period sitting across

from that person, what has changed? Does the agent in distress "want" to move. Or is it a "need"? For it to be a need, the manager must assume that there are other rational issues. A "need" is serious. So, if the agent tells the supervisor that he "needs" to move because of an allergic reaction to the perfume or cologne the agent in the seat next to him is wearing, that "need" becomes more valid than the "want".

5. The supervisor should relay some options to the agent in a way that ensures buy-in will be established if a decision is made. Very often, veteran agents have a relationship with the supervisor that other, less established agents, don't have. Therefore, it is safe to communicate potential options to veteran agents with the understanding that nothing is set in stone and won't be set in stone without their buy-in. Lines such as the ones below should be relayed to the veteran agent to ensure recognition on their part.

"You know how things have worked here in the past, don't you? With that in mind...."

"I don't want to mislead you because you have established yourself here at an extremely high level."

"I am extremely sensitive to what you are saying because I know you well."

6. The supervisor should probe for other issues or concerns that may arise. Veteran agents seem to have more issues than new or mid-level agents because they feel a comfort level with their boss and the company that others don't. Top agents also provide information to the supervisor that new and mid-level agents don't. When a meeting ensues about issues, the supervisor should take advantage of the time and find out what other thoughts the agent might have about his work. Top agents are far too valuable to lose track of, and any meeting is a good time to explore future issues.

7. The supervisor should provide the agent with reminders and examples of the agent's past successes. The supervisor should try to provide pictures and images from the past that will help in moving the agent out of her doldrums. We very often forget how good we are, or have been. It's our past success that motivates us to succeed further. As a supervisor, I very often can't recall momentous events that happened just last year, much less four or five years before. When I remember those positive events, it helps me to climb further in the present and,

if applicable, it brings me out of my doldrums. If we don't have time to think, reflect and act, certainly our agents are in the same boat.

8. The supervisor should schedule a follow-up visit. I learned quickly that making time for an agent who comes to you is good, but not great. Great is taking time out of your day to visit an agent who had come to you in the past.

Veteran agents have the understanding that they have excelled in the past. Therefore, they realize that they *can* do the job, however, they simply have hit a wall. A large part of working with veteran agents involves nurturing those agents. As veterans, they have established some rapport with their supervisors. That rapport requires nurturing. At the right time, in the right ways, management must be good enough to know how to spur a veteran agent to succeed. It may be by pushing the agent, or by backing away from the agent.

CHAPTER 9

Tips To Make Agents Successful

*"Attention is a strong aphrodisiac that
makes people want to do for other people."*
Dan Coen

Keep Agents On The Telephone

If your agent asks you why he isn't successful, ask your agent if he is staying on the telephone. The number one reason why struggling agents are not great at what they do is because struggling agents don't stay on the telephone. They don't recognize that extra breaks before and after their regular breaks quickly add up. For instance, track the number of breaks your agents take in a day. Then, analyze how your top, middle and low-end agents are performing in that day. Most patterns are very clear. The best agents stay on the telephone. They are disciplined to understand that selling or providing expert customer service is not a difficult proposition. Sales is a numbers game. Answering "X" amount of calls in a four or eight hour shift is also a numbers game. In a call center, numbers are accumulated by being mature enough to understand how the telephone is each agent's ally.

Bring Motivation To Each Agent In Simple Ways

Your agents feel compelled to succeed for you and themselves when you demonstrate how involved you are in their performance. So many agents are not used to attention. As we have discussed throughout this book, and will discuss further in the book, attention is a strong aphrodisiac that makes people want to do for other people. Simple examples include sitting down with an agent and spending five minutes talking to him about everything but work; handing an agent a note expressing your satisfaction with something he has done; giving an agent a dime, quarter or dollar bill to accompany a verbal form of motivation. Team contests do the trick as well. If a contest for the day has the whole team competing for five winning slots, there are five agents at the end of the day who will "win", thereby allowing you to build motivation upon the event.

Train

The least appreciated but most valued part of call center operations is the training of agents. Whether from the training department, or from the supervisor who designs a program specifically for a particular agent, training demonstrates partnership between agent and supervisor. Call center management must make it a point of training, and then implementing residual training. Computer training, product training and sales training must be a constant.

Make Goals Simple

Agents can meet and exceed simple goals. They can't meet or exceed goals they cannot understand. In the telesales and customer service environments, management must simplify exactly what they want from their agents. Then, they must communicate those goals clearly to their agents, and support those goals by managing around them.

Make Compensation Simple

Nothing destroys agent performance more than a compensation plan that is confusing. If your agents have no idea how they are getting paid, or how to read their primary pay sheets, then your call center must simplify the process. Many financial analysts develop the craziest compensation formulas because those numbers meet objectives. But, is that a practical compensation program for your agents to work from?

Provide Flexibility To Agents

By definition, agents recognize that their job is one built around structure. They must arrive at work at a certain time, work properly on the telephone, take lunch and breaks when appropriate. When management allows agents just a small amount of flexibility, they return the favor ten-fold. Flexibility may include leaving thirty minutes early, taking an extra break, etc.

Be Organized. Have A Daily Plan

When the supervisor has an organized, daily plan, results follow. Agents are only as responsible and as focused and as organized as their supervisor. If the supervisor is playing each day "by ear", agents will believe they can do the same.

Manage By Using Technology

In today's age, technology breeds opportunities for agents and supervisors. Supervisors can regularly track the number of seconds that customers wait in the queue. They can track whether an agent is talking, logged off, or not available to take calls. Most relevant, because supervisors have the tools, they merely need to utilize them. I am not a proponent of utilizing tools too often. Over-analyzing statistics takes the human element out of the equation. When that happens, agents don't respond, and supervisors don't succeed. But statistics via technology have an enormous place in the call center. By having an organized and consistent plan, supervisors can use technology to gauge the correct performance points of their agents. Agents become conditioned to perform based on the technology at hand. For instance, if an agent appears to be taking long lunches, the supervisor can use technology and statistics to "show" the agent in no uncertain terms that this is true. The agent's behavior pattern will become conditioned to respond to the fact that the supervisor can track lunch patterns.

CHAPTER 10

Using Class Categories To Better Manage Agents

"Grouping agents by who they are and what makes them tick will only help them, and the company, have a more solid foundation."

Dan Coen

In order to effectively communicate and motivate, supervisors must make it a point of recognizing that call center agents are grouped in classes. In essence, I am promoting responsible management by encouraging supervisors to take their team of agents and divide them into categories. I am urging supervisors to acknowledge that the way to truly manage agents is to divide them, label them and manage them based on who they are and what those divisions say about them.

Here is what supervisors first say when they hear me preach this. They disagree about grouping their agents in classes because they feel they are thereby favoring one agent over another. I hear supervisors tell me "I can't do that because I don't play favorites. I treat all my agents equally." To refute that, however, I want to remind supervisors that grouping agents in accordance with their skill sets, production attainments, experience with the company, and chemistry with peers does not mean the supervisor is playing favorites or choosing sides. Grouping agents by who they are and what makes them tick will only help them, and the company, have a more solid foundation. The supervisor is merely demonstrating intelligence by finding better ways to influence and manage the extensive array of personalities and professionals on the telephone. By acknowledging class separation in the call center, supervisors are also practicing the theories and realities of management that break records in the call center. We will explore these theories and realities in this section and define agent distinctions.

Here is the central concept of class separation. Instead of managing people in a straight line as if they were all the same, the supervisor improves his own and his agents' performance by being better and more successful in time management, team structure and goal orientation. This is accomplished by understanding the separate level that each agent is at. In that way, the supervisor will be able to get the most out of each person. Each agent will perform better when he is supervised at his own level by a manager who understands his specific needs.

Therefore, although each agent fundamentally must be treated fairly in relation to others, agents are nothing more than people in a group environment. By that definition, they fall into classes. For example, throughout the American Civil War, combatants were nothing more than people in a group environment, so they were placed in classes and sub- classes to be managed in a better way. Many citizens in the North fought for the Union, and subcategories developed from there. Some fought, some farmed, some wrote, some fled. All the citizens supporting the Union fell into cliques, and were treated that way. Farmers were not treated the same as soldiers, and students were not treated like farmers. Classes developed to better manage the operation of the war. In the army, each person had a role, and was supervised in accordance with that role. Some were generals, others lieutenants, and still others were sergeants and privates. Each rank was supervised according to their job requirements and skill levels.

Supervisors must be realistic in recognizing that all classes of agents can't be managed in the same way. A call center agent with six years of experience cannot be communicated with and influenced in the same way as a new agent with less than six months on the job. A call center agent who has never met his goals cannot be managed like a call center agent who always exceeds his goals. When managing a group of agents on a daily basis, supervisors must know which ones to motivate, which ones to communicate with, which ones to perform monitoring checklists with, and which ones to have private conferences with.

Additionally, supervisors must recognize that agents understand they are divided into classes, even though they won't mention it or promote it outright. In fact, unbeknownst to supervisors, agents do promote their class to other agents, away from management. Agents brag consistently about how motivated they are by their work or their supervisors, or how strong a relationship they feel they have with one supervisor or another. Those agents have selectively placed themselves in a class. Other agents gripe about how disappointed they are with their manager, their job performance, or their work situation. When agents do this, they are also developing a class. Veteran agents understand they won't receive monitoring checklists as often as do new or struggling agents. Fledgling agents who have yet to find a comfort zone recognize they should receive more attention from management. Agents understand that intelligent management will take the time to group them into classes.

Human Classification

Your call center can be broken down to include several human classes of agents. Imagine your call center as New York City in the early 20th Century. This melting pot accepted immigrants from all over the world, thereby establishing the United States as a cultural leader. Your call center is a melting pot of agents as well. In fact, every call center has over a dozen classes of agents, if not more. The following is a breakdown of the various classes. Do any of these categories cover as many as 90% of your agents?

1. High Maintenance Agent

High and Low maintenance agents are the first two classes of agents every supervisor must identify and learn to deal with. I define a high maintenance agent as one that always has issues, criticisms, questions and input regarding any imaginable topic. A high maintenance agent is the type of agent who brings any issue to the supervisor's attention; even issues that probably shouldn't be considered issues. We may know high maintenance agents as agents who complain about the temperature, the data in the computer, the customers, the computer screen emitting radiation, the challenges of the job, the chair, the compensation plan, the headset manufacturer, a peer department, payroll, friends and enemies in the call center, what those friends and enemies in the call center do on the telephone and at break, the fairness of contests, the fairness of prizes, the fairness of promotions, etc. High Maintenance agents are agents we usually can't live without, because they demonstrate accountability and caring with regard to their jobs. They take pride in their work, and they work admirably. Therefore, in spite of all the complaining supervisors may do about their high maintenance agents, supervisors will be disappointed when these agents move on. High Maintenance agents are inquisitive by nature, and passionate about everything. They also tend to be sensitive and emotional. For instance, the same sentence communicated in the same way by the supervisor on three different days will entice "HM" to respond in three completely different ways. High Maintenance agents are tough agents to manage. When "HM" comes to you with feedback on a particular topic, you must immediately recognize that you should react very slowly and thoughtfully. With "HM" agents, the way they feel can change so quickly that the way you respond is critical. You may give an "HM" agent what he says he wants only to cause more troubles with the "HM" agent the next day, or with peers of the "HM" agent who are unhappy with your decision. High Maintenance agents are the reason a supervisor gets his pay check.

2. Low Maintenance Agent

The exact opposite of a high maintenance agent is a low maintenance agent. These agents see the "big picture" in the call center. They recognize how challenging a supervisor's job can be. Low Maintenance agents have been through the mill, and recognize the value of their job. They are extremely consistent in their communication habits. They think before acting, and tend to portray the same disposition each day. When agent feedback takes place with low maintenance agents, the supervisor recognizes that he may be able to react and provide a fair solution to issues before those issues become a problem. Low Maintenance agents are self-starters and tend to display a maturity that makes the supervisor's job quite easy.

3. Attention-Driven Agent

The attention-driven agent is a sub-set of the high maintenance agent. The attention-driven agent wants to be seen by everybody in the call center. This agent may call the supervisor four or five times in a day simply to ask questions that have no relevance. He may throw birthday parties, holiday celebrations and other events simply to be involved in the process of the call center. Sometimes, he will be substituting involvement at work for a lack of involvement at home. Attention-Driven agents care about how they are perceived by their peers. They want to do the right things, and they want management to recognize they are doing the right things. They want their peers to commend them on their performances.

4. Authority-Pleasing Agent

The authority-pleasing agent is a sub-set of the high maintenance agent. The authority-pleasing agent wants to be seen by their supervisor as often as possible. This agent may call the supervisor four or five times in a day simply to ask questions that have no relevance, or to obtain simple answers the agent may have been able to find on her own. Authority-Pleasing agents care about how they are perceived by those in power. They want to do the right things, and they want management to recognize they are doing the right things.

5. Aloof Agent

The aloof agent is the introvert who would not be a successful outside sales representative. One of the reasons that agents choose inside sales over outside sales is that inside sales provide a curtain of anonymity that outside selling does not. Aloof Agents care about doing the job well. They don't want to be absorbed in the machinations of call center operations. They may participate in activities as a secondary figure, but they are more than likely to decline an invitation to join in events.

6. Paranoid Agent

The paranoid agent always believes that trouble in on the horizon. Paranoid agents spend as much time as possible fretting about the gloom and doom of myths and realities. For example, paranoid agents tend to spread gossip and start rumors about potential layoffs, new compensation plans, management changes, product adjustments, and so forth. Supervisors should take note that paranoid agents are the most fun to work with in the call center, because they are the easiest to manipulate!

7. Unhappy Agent

The unhappy agent should get another job elsewhere. Unhappy agents are almost always veterans in your call center. They may be unhappy about not advancing, about compensation, about the way they are supervised, etc., or they may be unhappy as a way of gaining attention. An unhappy agent can destroy a culture. Usually, however, they bring forth most of their disappointments upon themselves.

8. Consistent Performing Agent

The consistent performing agent is the agent that every supervisor enjoys managing. This category is a sub-set of the low maintenance agent. They understand the foundation of their job; they recognize what their role is in the call center; they always meet and exceed company objectives; they rarely pose a problem to management without offering some sort of support or solution to the issue. Consistent Performing agents see the big picture. They enjoy their jobs.

9. Job Performance in Jeopardy Agent

This is an agent who is on a performance development program. Every call center has agents who are not meeting objectives. They may still need to be talked with, or perhaps they have been spoken to and are on a performance plan. In either case, these are the agents who can see that their careers may come to an end soon.

10. "Why Did We Hire This Person" Agent

Every management team has a list of agents who are on the "why did we hire this person list". The agent may not show up to work on time, or may be painfully non-qualified for the role. In new hire training, the agent may lack simple communication skills, or even fall asleep in class. On the floor, the agent may contribute nothing, in any arena, to the call center.

11. Authority-Challenging Agent

This is a supervisor's worst nightmare. The authority-challenging agent is a sub-set of the high maintenance agent. However, the authority-challenging agent doesn't take "no" for an answer. They always believe their actions or ideas are worthy of full implementation. They spend time pitting one supervisor against another, and one supervisor's decisions against his boss' decisions. Authority-Challenging agents want to know <u>why</u>. They continually look for avenues to find a path to get their own way. They pit peers and management against one another for their own good.

12. Super Achiever Agent

This agent is a spectacular employee who does everything well. These don't come around very often.

13. Energizer Agent

This agent has a high energy level that contributes enormously to the culture of the call center. The energizer agent is a doer who cares about his position and the position of the company. They are the agents who volunteer to go shopping for food or contest prizes if necessary. They may spend hours after work designing programs to help the call center succeed.

Once management has identified what human classification each agent falls within, management can better supervise employees. For instance, when agent Y shows up at the supervisor's door, the supervisor should immediately identify what different classes he falls into. Is this a high maintenance agent with a tendency to be paranoid and attention-driven, or is this agent a low maintenance agent with consistent performance and an energizing disposition?

CHAPTER 11

Using American History To Develop Creative Communication Culture

"There is no terror in a bang, only in the anticipation if it."
Alfred Hitchcock

Time after time, call center executives ask me to assist them to develop a program to turn their operations around. In essence, they want to take their present environment and turn it inside out. Most of the time, management recognizes they have an operation that is under-performing. At the same time, they understand that telling agents to do better isn't always going to get the job done. Perhaps the management staff is not doing what they need to be doing. Or, agents don't feel as if they are making a contribution to the company, and it shows in their performance. Diving into a "change" in operations isn't about making something different simply to show that action is taking place. Thought before action is required. Creativity and risk-taking is encouraged.

History And The Founding Fathers

One merely needs to look through the prism of history to learn how to impact your call center environment. History is a truly spectacular guide, because history involves people who have created and administered events similar to your own. Therefore, one can recognize what should happen, what will happen and what can happen when one takes a moment to analyze what has happened in the past. How can call center supervisors bring history to their call centers? At the very least, it is a good idea for supervisors to attend a minimum of two outside call center conferences every year in order to gain practical ideas and insights into how they can better themselves and their environment. These conferences are made up of speakers who have succeeded in one arena or the other in the past. There is no reason to create the wheel when the wheel already exists. It is merely important to take the wheel and make it suit your world. This is the guide that history can give to a person.

When I sit down to develop a new environment for a call center, I rely on the successful foundation established by our founding fathers many centuries ago. In order to take your agents and form them into a dynamite unit of success that breaks records, I suggest you take a tip from our founding fathers and adopt the structure, objectives and processes that they used when they went about forming a country. Our founding fathers did many magnificent things hundreds of years ago. They failed in some areas, too, but the failures have been overshadowed by the brilliance of their organizational structures and philosophies. In a land that was, at the time, dominated by the only country they had ever known (England), in a world weeks of travel away from their mother country, they gathered together in the heat of a Philadelphia summer to develop a working document that would guide a country through an infinite number of years. In essence, they attempted to form a government that would do for people what their present government was not doing. Failure would result in charges of treason. And, they hoped their articles would be solid enough, and practical enough, to ensure that what had happened to them in the past would never happen to people on that continent again. When one thinks back to all the challenges and decisions that had to be made in order to form a powerful country, one realizes that facing challenges and making decisions to form and operate a powerful call center really isn't that much of a daunting task after all.

> The founding fathers set a precedent for how to operate a country, and a call center.

There are a few principles I use when creating, or recreating, call centers. First, the founding fathers succeeded in creating the United States because they began with a solid foundation. If a government is formed on a shaky foundation, history tells us that coups, military takeovers and political instability make that country a terrifying land in which to live. I figure that call centers must function under the same general philosophy. A solid foundation must be established before any other task begins. In the first ten years of the former Soviet Union, democracy struggled because the political leaders could not agree on a basic operating philosophy. Crime became outrageous. Freedoms, while implied, were curbed. The legislative branches of government (Congress) and executive branch (President) were never able to agree on the principles that could guide the country. Second, I have learned through studying our founding fathers that they took the initiative to provide proper organization and opportunities to their citizens, through their solid foundation. When governments present themselves as working for their people, people give their governments the support to keep moving forward. Through the channels of elections, referendums, town meetings and general consensus, those that do for those who need have the chance to continue to do. I have come to the conclusion that call centers can function the same way for their employees. Those call centers that make it a point of creating a strong operations base and a tremendous environment on behalf of their employees are usually the call centers that reap the rewards. Third, I discovered that our founding fathers created a solid working government because citizens are able to view clearly, through verbal communication and written documentation, the channels of organization and opportunity that have given them incentive to do better. When citizens see the vision, the vision becomes a reality. I feel it is paramount that this same philosophy transcends to the call center world as well.

Franklin Delano Roosevelt recreated the country in the same way management must go about recreating the call center. To place this in context, FDR became President in 1933, one of the most disheartening times in our nation's history. Unemployment was as high as 25%. Banks had collapsed, supermarkets had faltered, money was scarce, real estate had been lost. The great depression was destroying the moral fabric of the United States, while threatening democracy as a way of life. Our country was in trouble. Roosevelt's task was to do anything he could to bring America out of its doldrums. Roosevelt was able to put in place a working foundation that sustained America for the nine years before America encountered the social and emotional battle that was World War Two. More importantly, FDR rebuilt America and recreated the ways of life in the United States. After the second world war; after the depression had ended and society was moving forward; after the death of FDR; our country had built a wonderful structure of opportunity for all Americans that begins with the advent of social security and continues with the government's guarantee of banks, the GI Bill, and dozens of other programs that touch our world over 70 years later. Most importantly, FDR was able to raise the people of the United States from the depths of despair. FDR was able to take Desire, Concept and Initiative and bring out success.

"No other President had so thoroughly occupied the imagination of the American people. Using the new medium of the radio, he spoke directly to them, using simple words and everyday analogies, in a series of "fireside chats", designed not only to shape, educate and move public opinion forward but also to inspire people to act, make them participants in a shared drama. People felt he was talking to them personally, not to millions of others."

"After his first address on the banking crisis, in which he explained to families why it was safer to return their money to the banks rather than keep it at home, large deposits began flowing back in to the banking system. When he asked everyone to spread a map before them in preparation for a fireside chat on the war in the Pacific, map stores sold more maps in a span of days than they had in an entire year."

(Time Magazine. 12/31/99. Doris Kearns Goodwin. Page 100.)

Management must form a sound foundation and lead by example. Similar to a basketball coach who enters a basketball game with a game plan, I believe strongly that any call center executive who wants to bring about change in the call center must have a strategy in place to do just that. Taking from our nation's history, I utilize the Declaration of Independence and Bill of Rights as a format to make call centers excel.

Bringing these documents to the call center breathes new life into the policies and procedures, agents, supervisors, support staff, and ways that business is done on an everyday basis. They cause us to reassess the vision, practices and strengths of the call center from top to bottom. They create a structural foundation for the entire call center that would withstand any earthquake.

What our founding fathers did hundreds of years ago can be replicated and adapted to make the call center thrive. Our founding fathers recognized that if their foundation was solid and their strategy strong, in the long run a large majority of the people would be pleased with their own separate union. This foundation was developed through creation of the Declaration of Independence, and the strategy was procured through the Bill of Rights. The founding fathers certainly believed that if their form of government was successful, descendents for centuries to come would benefit from their great works. And so we have.

When anything different is presented in the call center, a typical reaction will ensue. Some agents will buy in and support the change, defying conditioning and embracing change. These agents will spread the news. To be successful today is important, but to become successful for our descendants is even more valuable. Nothing can be finer than to leave a company in better shape today and in better shape for the future. That is what all call centers require. That is what the people should strive for.

Bringing a Declaration of Independence and Bill of Rights to the call center is the first step in an action plan to develop a vision and a foundation for your call center. It is the channel to embrace positive change. When fresh ideas or new changes are desired, my experience has been that management recognizes they must make important changes in their call center for their call center to live. Yet, although they do desire fresh ideas and new changes, that same management team generally does not understand how to successfully make those changes. Sure, they can do a little here, or a little there. But eventually, a new emergency or idea comes to the forefront and any attempt at change is forgotten. Change is simply too difficult.

In this vein, management gurus will be the first to tell struggling organizations that their companies lack vision, and that a simple mission statement won't be enough to fix that. "Vision" is another one of those overused and irritating words that you see in books and that you hear in conferences all of the time. "Your employees don't see a vision" or "Your department has no vision" or "Your company has a mixed up vision of what they want to do". Yet, the word does have true meaning. Why tinker around with a great word when the word says everything you need it to say? When one looks at a struggling call center in need of action, one can usually find a lack of vision from the top down. Agents don't feel comfortable that they know what is going on in the call center. Supervisors can't describe areas that would elicit comfort. Upper management fails to articulate a course, strategy, or goals. The call center is a living unit of action with little motivation to move anywhere. There is no overriding vision. Nobody feels accountable. Nobody has written and verbal explanations of where everybody wants to be.

When I speak with supervisors, managers, directors, vice presidents and CEO's, they readily admit that their call center could do a better job of promoting a vision, and inspiration, for its employees. Sometimes they see that problem as their issue, a management issue, because they and management haven't addressed what they want to demonstrate as vision and inspiration in the first place. Oftentimes, the practice of developing the vision and inspiration is an intangible that management can't get their hands around. In essence, they understand they need to make something happen for their employees, departments and the business as a whole. They just don't know how to do it. They recognize a mission statement is valuable, but they also know that a mission statement will be nothing more than a jumbled set of words which mean absolutely nothing unless it is put into action and utilized to the success of everyone involved. Where management falters is not in its recognition of the issue, but in its planning and implementation of the mission. The Declaration of Independence and Bill of Rights can solve much of that when applied correctly.

> Citizens have been able to view clearly, through verbal communication and written documentation, how government works.

Take a moment and think about your call center, its departments and its employees as they are today. Do they live, breathe and promote the vision of your company each day? Review your vision for your business. Do your employees even know what it is, and do they see in real terms how they can make a difference in promoting that vision? Is there a call center vision? Most cognitively, analyze the foundation of your department, the organization and opportunities that live in your call center, and the written and verbal communications that provide support. Do they make sense? Is there a structure that falls into place? Is there a pattern that leads all employees to successful venues? Is there a system to the madness? Is there a foundation?

Whether your answer is "yes" or "no", review the following three simple results that a Declaration of Independence and Bill of Rights can bring to your call center. Ask yourself if your call center needs to make headway in any of these areas.

1. They will bring organization, vision and direction to the call center. Management doesn't make an impact when all they do is verbalize changes. History taught that our founding fathers didn't just create a country. They created a system that rules the country. These two documents will provide the basis so that management and agents may join forces and create a more perfect call center that will ensure that company objectives are met.

2. They will help to create a whole new climate of energy in the call center. Agents and supervisors will want to be on teams in order to contribute to a new world. Other departments will ask for copies of what is being done so they may mimic the call center, and they will ask for notes after any meeting so they may obtain a working guide. In short, an energy, buzz, excitement and purpose will take shape in the call center. People will become excited about the potential for a new operating structure. They also will become excited because they can be a part of the process of implementing a new operating structure. The energy and focus in the company during this developmental process will be unprecedented. Employees will feel that they are contributing to their own success. Involvement will spread like wildfire.

3. The development of these documents will increase results and dramatically improve production, implement a culture of superior management and motivation. Supervisors will stop agent turnover, and provide a guide that every employee can use for years to come.

Initial Steps To Create A Declaration of Independence And Bill Of Rights

The Declaration of Independence and the Bill of Rights are nothing more than stories. Like any story, there is an introduction, a detailed presentation, and a conclusion. In television soap operas, a story may last years and decades. In movies, stories last about two and a half hours. Our founding fathers created a story that has lasted into parts of four different centuries.

What is the story of your call center? What are the objectives of creating a new communication culture within your call center?

The first step is to form an organizational structure that will ensure the proceedings go well. Get down to the basics first. For instance, there must be note-takers and leads who document clearly what happens every step of the way, and it is required that somebody run the proceedings. When the constitutional convention took shape, the primary note-taker for the event was James Madison. He sat in the front row each day and furiously took notes on every action. Through those notes, historians have been able to determine how our country and its government was formed. The lead was George Washington, who was unanimously elected to guide the proceedings. One person must take the lead and be in charge of any development. In your call center, duties need to be assigned, teams need to be established, and roles need to be delegated and organized. But one person needs to be the figure who brings everything together. Once that one person is chosen, it is his responsibility to contract a team that will administer the process. This team may be made up of any number of people so long as the group as a whole possesses the correct dynamic to effect change. In addition, regular meetings must be planned. Whether you are able to meet for one week straight or three times each month, some sort of calendar must be created.

Declaration of Independence

The Declaration of Independence provides the rationale for making some changes in your call center. Traditionally, the senior manager or CEO of the company may call a meeting and introduce urgency in development of new ideas, values, and practices. Before that, however, must come a written agenda. In the call center, verbal proclamations can easily get lost in the shuffle. What a senior leader says on a Monday is forgotten two Mondays forward. Documentation must be established to keep all team personnel clearly up-to-date on proceedings. The Declaration of Independence was originally written by Thomas Jefferson. It is the document that founded our country and laid out step by step reasons why the original thirteen colonies were seceding from England. Your goal in writing a Declaration of Independence for your call center is to lay out in complete detail the reasons your call center must change direction, reform operations and improve performance. The Declaration of Independence for your call center sets forth problems in the call center. It delves into any and all working relationships. It talks about what your call center wants to do, and needs to do, to succeed under a new system. Most importantly, it provides the reasoning for *why* a change is being undertaken.

Your Declaration of Independence is a summary / background as to why your call center needs to declare independence from what it is presently doing today. Perhaps agents need to declare independence from poor performance on the telephones, arriving late to work, and taking extra long breaks. Perhaps supervision needs to make a Declaration of Independence from managing agents with an iron fist, and not allowing agents to take breaks when they choose to. Perhaps the Declaration of Independence announces that the call center will take a step away from promoting a poor culture, and instead will be intent on building a climate that stresses opportunities and compassion.

History tells us that Thomas Jefferson penned the Declaration of Independence on his own, with guidance from his peers. I recommend the manager in charge pen the document, but begin the process by convening groups of fellow management personnel, a mix of agents, and various department peers to provide insight. Don't do it alone! That goes against the whole philosophy of this project! In addition, history shows that the Declaration of Independence was written to motivate and persuade the citizens of the original thirteen colonies to act, in verbal action and physical revolution. From Washington to Adams to Hamilton and Jefferson, our founding fathers knew that without the Declaration of Independence, there would be little rationale for starting a revolution against a mother country.

Below is the Declaration of Independence, drafted by Thomas Jefferson between June 11 and June 28, 1776. Following that is a sample Declaration of Independence I have developed to illustrate the type of declaration your call center may one day develop.

IN CONGRESS, July 4, 1776.

The unanimous Declaration of the thirteen United States of America,

When in the Course of human events, it becomes necessary for one people to dissolve the political bands which have connected them with another, and to assume among the powers of the earth, the separate and equal station to which the Laws of Nature and of Nature's God entitle them, a decent respect to the opinions of mankind requires that they should declare the causes which impel them to the separation.

We hold these truths to be self-evident, that all men are created equal, that they are endowed by their Creator with certain inalienable Rights, that among these are Life, Liberty and the pursuit of Happiness.—That to secure these rights, Governments are instituted among Men, deriving their just powers from the consent of the governed, —That whenever any Form of Government becomes destructive of these ends, it is the Right of the People to alter or to abolish it, and to institute new Government, laying its foundation on such principles and organizing its powers in such form, as to them shall seem most likely to effect their Safety and Happiness. Prudence, indeed, will dictate that Governments long established should not be changed for light and transient causes; and accordingly all experience hath shewn, that mankind are more disposed to suffer, while evils are sufferable, than to right themselves by abolishing the forms to which they are accustomed. But when a long train of abuses and usurpations, pursuing invariably the same Object evinces a design to reduce them under absolute Despotism, it is their right, it is their duty, to throw off such Government, and to provide new Guards for their future security.—Such has been the patient sufferance of these Colonies; and such is now the necessity which constrains them to alter their former Systems of Government. The history of the present King of Great Britain is a history of repeated injuries and usurpations, all having in direct object the establishment of an absolute Tyranny over these States. To prove this, let Facts be submitted to a candid world.

He has refused his Assent to Laws, the most wholesome and necessary for the public good.

He has forbidden his Governors to pass Laws of immediate and pressing importance, unless suspended in their operation till his Assent should be obtained; and when so suspended, he has utterly neglected to attend to them.

He has refused to pass other Laws for the accommodation of large districts of people, unless those people would relinquish the right of Representation in the Legislature, a right inestimable to them and formidable to tyrants only.

He has called together legislative bodies at places unusual, uncomfortable, and distant from the depository of their public Records, for the sole purpose of fatiguing them into compliance with his measures.

He has dissolved Representative Houses repeatedly, for opposing with manly firmness his invasions on the rights of the people.

He has refused for a long time, after such dissolutions, to cause others to be elected; whereby the Legislative powers, incapable of Annihilation, have returned to the People at large for their exercise; the State remaining in the mean time exposed to all the dangers of invasion from without, and convulsions within.

He has endeavoured to prevent the population of these States; for that purpose obstructing the Laws for Naturalization of Foreigners; refusing to pass others to encourage their migrations hither, and raising the conditions of new Appropriations of Lands.

He has obstructed the Administration of Justice, by refusing his Assent to Laws for establishing Judiciary powers.

He has made Judges dependent on his Will alone, for the tenure of their offices, and the amount and payment of their salaries.

He has erected a multitude of New Offices, and sent hither swarms of Officers to harass our people, and eat out their substance.

He has kept among us, in times of peace, Standing Armies without the Consent of our legislatures.

He has affected to render the Military independent of and superior to the Civil power.

He has combined with others to subject us to a jurisdiction foreign to our constitution, and unacknowledged by our laws; giving his Assent to their Acts of pretended Legislation:

For Quartering large bodies of armed troops among us:

For protecting them, by a mock Trial, from punishment for any Murders which they should commit on the Inhabitants of these States:

For cutting off our Trade with all parts of the world:

For imposing Taxes on us without our Consent:

For depriving us in many cases, of the benefits of Trial by Jury:

For transporting us beyond Seas to be tried for pretended offences

For abolishing the free System of English Laws in a neighboring Province, establishing therein an Arbitrary government, and enlarging its Boundaries so as to render it at once an example and fit instrument for introducing the same absolute rule into these Colonies:

For taking away our Charters, abolishing our most valuable Laws, and altering fundamentally the Forms of our Governments:

For suspending our own Legislatures, and declaring themselves invested with power to legislate for us in all cases whatsoever.

He has abdicated Government here, by declaring us out of his Protection and waging War against us.

He has plundered our seas, ravaged our Coasts, burnt our towns, and destroyed the lives of our people.

He is at this time transporting large Armies of foreign Mercenaries to complete the works of death, desolation and tyranny, already begun with circumstances of Cruelty & perfidy scarcely paralleled in the most barbarous ages, and totally unworthy the Head of a civilized nation.

He has constrained our fellow Citizens taken Captive on the high Seas to bear Arms against their Country, to become the executioners of their friends and Brethren, or to fall themselves by their Hands.

He has excited domestic insurrections amongst us, and has endeavored to bring on the inhabitants of our frontiers, the merciless Indian Savages, whose known rule of warfare, is an undistinguished destruction of all ages, sexes and conditions.

In every stage of these Oppressions We have Petitioned for Redress in the most humble terms: Our repeated Petitions have been answered only by repeated injury. A Prince whose character is thus marked by every act which may define a Tyrant, is unfit to be the ruler of a free people.

Nor have We been wanting in attentions to our British brethren. We have warned them from time to time of attempts by their legislature to extend an unwarrantable jurisdiction over us. We have reminded them of the circumstances of our emigration and settlement here. We have appealed to their native justice and magnanimity, and we have conjured them by the ties of our common kindred to disavow these usurpation's, which, would inevitably interrupt our connections and correspondence. They too have been deaf to the voice of justice and of consanguinity. We must, therefore, acquiesce in the necessity, which denounces our Separation, and hold them, as we hold the rest of mankind, Enemies in War, in Peace Friends.

We, therefore, the Representatives of the united States of America, in General Congress, Assembled, appealing to the Supreme Judge of the world for the rectitude of our intentions, do, in the Name, and by Authority of the good People of these Colonies, solemnly publish and declare, That these United Colonies are, and of Right ought to be Free and Independent States; that they are Absolved from all Allegiance to the British Crown, and that all political connection between them and the State of Great Britain, is and ought to be totally dissolved; and that as Free and Independent States, they have full Power to levy War, conclude Peace, contract Alliances, establish Commerce, and to do all other Acts and Things which Independent States may of right do. And for the support of this Declaration, with a firm reliance on the protection of divine Providence, we mutually pledge to each other our Lives, our Fortunes and our sacred Honor. (**National Archives and Records Administration**) (http://www.nara.gov/exhall/charters/declaration/decmain.html)

CALL CENTER DECLARATION OF INDEPENDENCE (SAMPLE)

When in the course of this ever-changing call center world of business and technology, it becomes necessary for people combined together to dissolve the professional bonds which have connected them and begin the process to create anew a dynamic new environment of opportunity, they should declare the causes that impel them to first dissolve and then create their new environment.

We hold these truths to be self-evident, that all agents are created equal, that they are endowed by management and supervision with certain inalienable rights, that among these rights are opportunities to flourish in their environment, a positive culture geared to promote their success, continuous training to assist them in their endeavors, and a fair and impartial management team focused on creating teamwork and partnership as their number one objective.

Whenever any operational foundation fails to create an opportunity that breeds success for all parties therein, it is the right of management with assistance from the very agents they represent to alter the present operations structure and institute a new foundation, laying its foundation on such principles and organizing its environment in such form as to all parties shall seem most likely to effect the entire businesses' happiness and prosperity. Prudence, indeed, will dictate that the operating foundations shall not be changed for light and transient causes; change occurs when the business need, operating foundation and culture of the call center dictates that a change in vision will bring forth grand opportunity and success for the business and its team members as a whole.

The history of the present operating structure is one that is not succeeding to the levels the present management team desires. To prove this, let facts be submitted:

(List 10 or more aspects of the call center that need reorganization)

1.

2.

3.

4.

5.

6.

7.

8.

9.

10.

We, therefore, the management team, do solemnly publish and declare that this call center will renew itself to create an exciting business model and an operating foundation for present and future management and agents to thrive under. One that, when teaming together with all call center personnel, will create a culture of opportunity that brings financial, emotional and professional success to the call center and its people within.

Bill of Rights

The Declaration of Independence introduces why change needs to be made, along with some of the aspects of change that management deems valuable. In the Bill of Rights section, management and agent must work together to generate as many amendments as they wish to begin the process of change. The objective: To set a foundation that impacts all personnel and procedures in the call center. What must be implemented to turn the call center around? The Bill of Rights is the core foundation of change and action in your call center. It sets forth the policies and procedures of the call center. These Bill of Rights are the commitments that management and agents will make to one another. Your Bill of Rights sets the ground rules. Below is the original ten Bill of Rights, drafted by the United States Congress as an addendum to the Constitution. Following that is a sample Bill of Rights I have developed to illustrate the type of goals your call center may one day develop.

Amendment I

Congress shall make no law respecting an establishment of religion, or prohibiting the free exercise thereof; or abridging the freedom of speech, or of the press; or the right of the people peaceably to assemble, and to petition the Government for a redress of grievances.

Amendment II

A well regulated Militia, being necessary to the security of a free State, the right of the people to keep and bear Arms, shall not be infringed.

Amendment III

No Soldier shall, in time of peace be quartered in any house, without the consent of the Owner, nor in time of war, but in a manner to be prescribed by law.

Amendment IV

The right of the people to be secure in their persons, houses, papers, and effects, against unreasonable searches and seizures, shall not be violated, and no Warrants shall issue, but upon probable cause, supported by Oath or affirmation, and particularly describing the place to be searched, and the persons or things to be seized.

Amendment V

No person shall be held to answer for a capital, or otherwise infamous crime, unless on a presentment or indictment of a Grand Jury, except in cases arising in the land or naval forces, or in the Militia, when in actual service in time of War or public danger; nor shall any person be subject for the same offence to be twice put in jeopardy of life or limb; nor shall be compelled in any criminal case to be a witness against himself, nor be deprived of life, liberty, or property, without due process of law; nor shall private property be taken for public use, without just compensation.

Amendment VI

In all criminal prosecutions, the accused shall enjoy the right to a speedy and public trial, by an impartial jury of the State and district wherein the crime shall have been committed, which district shall have been previously ascertained by law, and to be informed of the nature and cause of the accusation; to be confronted with the witnesses against him; to have compulsory process for obtaining witnesses in his favor, and to have the Assistance of Counsel for his defence.

Amendment VII

In suits at common law, where the value in controversy shall exceed twenty dollars, the right of trial by jury shall be preserved, and no fact tried by a jury, shall be otherwise reexamined in any Court of the United States, than according to the rules of the common law.

Amendment VIII

Excessive bail shall not be required, nor excessive fines imposed, nor cruel and unusual punishments inflicted.

Amendment IX

The enumeration in the Constitution, of certain rights, shall not be construed to deny or disparage others retained by the people.

Amendment X

The powers not delegated to the United States by the Constitution, nor prohibited by it to the States, are reserved to the States respectively, or to the people.

(http://www.nara.gov/exhall/charters/billrights/billrights.html)

(National Archives and Records Administration)

CALL CENTER BILL OF RIGHTS (SAMPLE)

Amendment I

Management shall make no rule prohibiting meetings between management and agents on topics of importance to any party. Management commits to the value of regular open communication amongst employees and staff. Management encourages agents to petition the company for a redress of grievances.

Amendment II

All call center policies and procedures, being necessary to the promotion of a quality call center, must be respected by agents, and shall not be infringed.

Amendment III

No agent shall be asked to perform duties for which they have not been trained on. This call center commits to quality training and organization for all employees.

Amendment IV

This call center encourages open contests, prizes and games. Management will ensure that every team in the call center has the ability to participate in programs that reward them for meeting attainable objectives.

Amendment V

Call Center agents agree that they will perform their duties to the best of their abilities within the course of their scheduled work hours.

Amendment VI

Management guarantees a wonderful work environment, with positive training, meetings and exterior environment that ensures the work environment is a fun place to be.

Amendment VII

In issues of disagreement between agents and supervisors, the right to meet with senior management shall be preserved. Management believes in a quality program to mediate disagreements in a sincere and timely manner.

Amendment VIII

Management and agents agree to work together to better the performance of projects. This means that when a project is not meeting its objectives, both parties will convene to better performance. This can be accomplished through training, assessment of fundamentals, etc.

Amendment IX

The enumeration in these Bill of Rights of certain rights shall not be construed to deny or disparage other rights retained by the agents and management.

Amendment X

Management and Agents reserve the right to work together to develop more Bill of Rights, and to amend those Bill of Rights already in place.

CHAPTER 12

Introducing Culture and Prosperity To Your Call Center

"Nothing is built on stone; all is built on sand, but we must build as if the sand were stone."
Jorge Luis Borges

Ask your staff this question. What if your culture was a little different? Not a grand change, mind you. Simply something other than what it presently is. For instance, imagine your department with different managers; perhaps management from other jobs you might have had. Put your present job, and your old managers, together. What do you see? What if your office were a bit bigger? How would that help? What if your headsets were more comfortable? Could your environment around you be better? What if your boss was nicer, or more strict, or less empathetic? Would that affect the way you perform in your job? Would that impact your daily mannerisms and outlook at your job?

I ask those who desire a world class culture to pause and imagine the environment of an amusement park such as Disneyland. Then, I ask them to incorporate many of the traits that make Disneyland special into their own professional work environment. At first glance, one may think I'm fuzzy in the brain to equate Disneyland and call centers. Disneyland is a fantasy theme park that promotes fun and escapism, while the call center is a reality-based work environment that normally promotes a daily grind of some form of capitalism. That's all somewhat true, but bear with me. The same principles that make the culture of Disneyland so successful can provide call center management with building blocks to build an equally successful operation.

When management becomes Goofy, Mickey and Donald in the call center, management brings to their agents the reasons to be successful. Those three images, and others like them, present messages to theme park visitors, and call center agents, on how to observe the theme park and call center. Unlike other sales departments, or other departments in a company, the call center presents a first-rate opportunity to be zany.

A call center can be a Disneyland if call center management desires to make it a Disneyland for their agents! The supervisors who strive to make their call center more like a Disneyland WIN day in and day out, because their agents WIN day in and day out. Those creative, unique, off the top call centers that search for ways to be more like "the happiest place on earth" are the ones that break records all of the time. Disneyland is only Disneyland because senior management chooses to make it the way it is. Your call center will become the exact way you choose it to become. A call center can be a Disneyland.

For instance, one of the aspects of Disneyland many people are not aware of when they go to Disneyland is the professional staff. Disneyland's professional staff works very hard to create entertainment for consumers like you and me. Among their objectives is to stay "out of the way" as much as possible. Although you don't see them when you don't choose to, you can find a staff member when you want one. When I think of Disneyland employees, I think of custodial crews making the place comfortable, and high school students in the summertime working the "Pirates of the Caribbean". I think of actors masquerading as famous Disney characters. And I think of courteous servers preparing meals and dispensing food during a sun-filled day. In the book The Disney Way, McGraw Hill, 1999, authors Bill Capodagli and Lynn Jackson capably explain that when it comes to the management of Disney, *"The Walt Disney Company is the master at creating controlled environments that never disappoint. Because the company goes to great lengths to communicate its beliefs and traditions to every cast member, the Disney product offers people a comforting familiarity that is hard to duplicate in today's fast-paced world."* (Pg. 196)

> Agents see their supervisors and interpret their mood, and, the mood of the call center culture.

With all the fun and excitement of a day at Disneyland, it is important to recognize that the staff of Disneyland attempts to portray a professional image all of the time. The custodian is as professional as the ticket-taker, and those who operate rides have the same friendly service approach as do the groundskeepers. When a guest contacts an employee, the employee is always responsive, even if he or she does not know the answer to a particular question. And the employees provide this responsiveness while dressed in costume, or in the middle of a job, or at the end of a long day. No matter what their title, all employees of Disneyland go through intensive customer service training before starting a job. They are required to be capable of managing the fun of a day at the park with the professional work involved. In essence, employees serve guests spectacularly well at Disneyland so guests can find enjoyment and success and come back for more. Why can't management serve call center agents so agents find enjoyment in their jobs and success on the telephones, so they will be motivated to come back for more as well?

"My Call Center Can Be A Disneyland"

Call centers are perfectly suited to become the Disneyland of your company. First, everybody who plays a part in making a call center successful should strive at all times to be professional and carry themselves with professional dignity. Second, everybody in a call center is likely to be a little bit off the wall and crazy anyhow, as they have chosen the call center environment as their place of employment. The accounting department cannot become a Disneyland. It just doesn't work. There isn't enough accent on communication and teamwork and personalities. Neither can outside field departments. They don't spend enough time in one place, together, like call center employees do. Outside employees sometimes see their office only once a week. In the call center, nobody ever goes anywhere. It's all confined.

One consistency I have found at every call center conference, show and meeting is that management and agents are in agreement that no person ever planned to be in the call center environment, growing up. Lawyers dream of their future profession as kids, and so do professional athletes. So do many firemen and police officers. But there are very few fourteen-year-olds who aspire to work in a call center. Therefore, management and agents of all types readily agree that there is a bond of impulsiveness that can be exploited in the call center.

In essence, there aren't very many companies or departments that can promote both professional employees and silly employees in an environment that capitalizes on this uniqueness. Can you imagine going to a meeting of your MIS / IT department in your company, and telling them that we are bringing the personality of a Disneyland into their culture? Positive feedback would be muted. But call center management **can**, and should, consider themselves capable of bringing Disneyland into their call center. Just like Disneyland employees do. And they should begin to take the principles and steps of Disneyland and transfer that uniqueness to the call center world.

Disneyland is most certainly an environment encompassing communication. Verbal communication from everybody in the park exists constantly from opening to closing. If one could capture every word spoken in the park during only one day, one would list millions and millions and millions of different words. The whole dictionary might be used. The same analogy exists with your call center.

Disneyland is a visual communication environment too. On any day there could be as many as 75,000 visitors. That's quite a bit to look at! Imagine taking a piece of paper and writing a note about every person you come in contact with. Thousands and thousands of people cross your path every hour in Disneyland. If only someone would give you $10 for each person who walked by, you probably wouldn't have to worry about work again! The same analogy exists with your call center.

More so than in any other culture, call center agents experience verbal communication all of the time. It can give an agent a headache. Call after call, verbal communication after verbal communication. After a call, the agent often receives more verbal communication from supervisors, or peers, or from other departments. The call center is first and foremost a verbal world.

The call center is a visual world, too. Agents see their computer and they see their peers. They imagine their customers and prospects on the telephone. They see mental pictures of the people they are speaking with. If lucky, or perhaps unlucky, agents see their supervisors, too. They see their supervisors happy, sad, stressed, calm, motivated, confused. They interpret what they see to mean something personal. "Did we as a call center world do something wrong, or right?" "Did I as an employee do something right, or wrong?"

The call center is the quintessential communication culture in the corporate work place. No other department can match the number of words, sounds and sights that take place in a call center on a given day. So if the call center is the quintessential communication place, then management needs to incorporate quintessential communication to ensure that their agents shine. Just like at Disneyland.

Costumes

Call Center managers should not be afraid to wear costumes in the call center, and to use the guise of costumes to create an organizational culture that introduces passion to its employees. If management takes this concept and runs with it, the call center becomes a world of opportunity.

Costumes define "performance" in nearly every setting. Actors in a play wear costumes to bring the play more credibility. Costumes represent fantasy by taking the actors and audience to a different place in time. The performance becomes authenticated. The same goes for sports (football and soccer players), politics (legislators), business (janitorial crews, CEO's, IT), education (teachers, principles, students), etc. Costumes distinguish roles, and help the players, and the people around the players, to better validate their production. Call Center management is the essence of performance. That's why costumes make all the difference. For instance, suppose your call center agents are divided into teams. Management can assign a consistent costume for each team. Every Friday, for example, may be designated as "costume day." A call center with seven teams may want to take the costume of a baseball team. Supervisors may dress up like the coaches of a team, and players wear uniform tops. There is a great opportunity to build contests, excitement, humor and performance expectations into this special day. Every hour might be an inning; every sale made can be a "run". Teams can compete against each other for the day. Prizes can be awarded. Other costumes can be based on television shows, other athletic sports, music groups, movies, etc.

When I observe a call center culture, I want to see costumes, or at least a distinction between teams, employees, and departments based on some fashion of costume. This may include hats, glasses, shoes, colors, wristbands, headbands, etc. Many supervisors fail to see the correlation between supervising agents on the telephone and wearing costumes. They don't have the personal gumption to wear costumes. They feel it's embarrassing. They see it as self-deprecating. These supervisors have failed to conceptualize the true impact that fantasy has in motivating and coaching agents. Supervisors who fail to wear costumes fail to see how costumes heighten performance. They also fail to remember that their job is a service- oriented job. Supervisors serve agents. In actuality, actors in a play could wear any outfit they chose to wear on stage — but a small fraction of their performance would be lost in the translation, not to mention a small fraction of character credibility. Costumes bring spirit to a call center. Costumes help to take a tangible objective and focus agents on meeting that objective. I have never seen call center agents fail to reach a goal on a day when our entire call center was dressed in costume. The agents and management were compelled to meet their objectives on that day. This is because costumes are very motivational.

Human beings dress up in costumes for two distinct purposes: to motivate the people around them, and to ensure that the people around them are getting the most from their environment. I have worn various masks and capes in many of the call centers I worked at. They were so motivational, and humorous to the call center agents that I developed contests around my costumes. For example, if we had less than five percent abandoned rate in our queue for a three day period, I would come in on Friday dressed in a costume, and we would give away prizes all centered around the theme of my costume. Believe me, this stuff works! If you have two agents or two hundred, you can motivate your agents by pretending to be something other than what you usually are. (Don't we do that every day?) Disappear and become a performer. Don't be afraid to swallow your pride, or ego, and let loose.

Costume Parameters

1. Don't wear costumes all of the time, or agents will become accustomed to it and it no longer becomes motivational.
2. Invite your agents to join you in costumes.
3. Wear costumes for a purpose. Perhaps there is a team contest.
4. Perhaps it's humorous motivation to keep agents compelled to perform. Have a purpose around your costumes.
5. Present prizes and awards based on the various themes of costumes.
6. Use costumes to increase spirit.
7. Do not be afraid to become the character that matches your costume.

Be Seen, Not Heard

Another example of turning your call center into a Disneyland, and hence a communication stage, involves being seen and not heard.

I do promote the concept that to motivate their agents, supervisors should be seen and not heard. That is what Disneyland employees do. They are always walking around, doing their jobs, always seen by guests. They never interrupt a conversation or communicate their points unless required to do so. They exist to assist, not to manipulate. (Side story. I was talking to a hotel employee and he was telling me his hotel had been debating two schools of thought. First theory: that every guest should be talked to, greeted, welcomed, and queried each time he or she set foot within a lobby. Second theory: that all employees should be available but not bothersome to the guests, so as not to get in the way. As you might imagine, I proposed a third school of thought. How about finding ways to ensure that the guest recognizes the employees are available without the employees getting in the guest's way.....hmmmm. Think creatively. This is exactly what they do at Disneyland. The security guards, for instance, are all dressed in various cast costumes. Guests recognize they are there, but they are not called upon unless needed.)

Always remember supervisors should be seen and not heard. Supervisors should think creatively. Supervisors should find ways to communicate their availability without getting in the way. Supervisors should be around.

It's The Fish

Here is an example of a motivational program that you may want to try in your call center.

In this story, our team was coming off a particularly fantastic month of March, and they were off to a slow start in April. This is quite predictable. Baseball teams that win ten games in a row oftentimes lose five games in a row after that. One streak begets another. Therefore, I wasn't very surprised when our performance for the first seven days of the month of April came nowhere close to duplicating our performance for the same period in the month of March. Every coach has to find ways to motivate his staff in different circumstances.

What I saw as I walked around the floor was that the agents were motivated on a low level; there was an undercurrent. I could sense they weren't nearly as energized about performing as they had been in the previous month. A few principles came to mind. I knew the agents were only slightly motivated even though they had goals to meet. I understood they were struggling because the month before was extremely positive, and it was a hard month to duplicate. They were trying to duplicate perfection, and flailing away at every turn. In addition, I could ascertain that they weren't energized because I wasn't energizing them like I did the month before. I was being part of the problem, not part of the solution. In essence, one of the problems in April is that I, like the agents, was so enthused with *last month's* performance that I wasn't focusing myself, and the team, on *this month's* performance.

> Supervisors who fail to wear costumes do not see the correlation that fantasy has in motivating and coaching agents. Costumes bring spirit to the call center!

To combat this, I walked around the floor and talked to the agents, successful and flailing alike. "How ya doing", "Tough day today", "Do you have plans for vacation soon", etc. The small talk that creates relationships gives a manager some good ideas. What I noted with regard to all the agents who were performing poorly was that they were dialing and trying and failing. There was pressure. Too much. What I noted regarding the few agents who were performing well was that they all had something in common. A fish. In this instance, they all had a fish bowl at their desk, with a fish swimming around inside.

It's the fish! I had my theme to motivate my agents. Because I had a theme, I could feel, quite succinctly, that a concept was coming around the corner. Like an emotional hurricane, quickly, I began walking around the call center floor, chanting "It's the fish, it's the fish". My agents already knew, due to past experiences, that I was a bit crazy anyhow, and they have come to expect sudden yelps and starts from me now and again. This was different. I went around and around the floor, chirping "It's the fish, it's the fish". The agents began asking me what I was talking about, and they began enjoying the display of intrigue. I could sense they were shooting e-mail's back and forth, saying something like "What in the world is Dan talking about?" Then, I began to hear the murmurs of a successful concept in its infancy.

"I had a tuna fish sandwich for lunch," one said, and a corner of the floor broke up in laughter. "I went fishing last week," exclaimed another.

I had my idea. It was late in the day, so I saved it for the next day. First, I sat at the computer after work and took ten minutes to draw up a perfect flier, with the headline boldly stating: "It's the fish". I made the flier colorful, and added motivational one liners and tips involving selling and meeting objectives, all in keeping with the theme that "It's the fish". I even mentioned in the flier that for the months of April and May, the theme would be: "It's the fish". Within ten minutes, I had a flier and 50 copies hot off the press, all on bright and cheery paper in various different colors.

That night, I went to the local supermarket and bought eighty cans of Tuna. Each can cost less than seventy cents. The next morning I arrived at work just twenty minutes early, went to each agent's desk, and placed one flier on each chair, with a can of tuna on the flier. I waited for my agents to arrive. They had their motivation.

Our best day of the year took place that day. After March, April turned into our second-best month of the year. All the agents were laughing and talking among themselves. They began chanting the same slogan: "It's the fish". Each time somebody was performing well, I asked them why, and they would invariably say: "It's the fish". Two years later, that flier still remained posted on all their cubicles.

Creative ideas in the call center don't have to be world-famous and insurmountable. Anybody with a little *desire* could have come up with that, or a similar idea. It's the *concept* that matters. I recognized the team needed motivation and I knew the team needed focus. I had to come up with a concept that would make this happen. Many of my other concepts might have worked, but, what is that saying: If you do the same old thing, you'll get the same old results? Instead, I let my mind roam as I roamed the call center, and I found one of a million correlation's that I could have used to have a fun contest. This correlation was the fish. It could have been perfume, or clothes, or hairdo.

Then, I gathered my *initiative* to make things happen. Ten minutes in front of the computer is just as good as painting a Rembrandt when it comes to the call center. Fifteen minutes in the grocery store is similar to spending a million dollars in prizes. That's what you need to make success.

Desire + Concept + Initiative =Simple Success

It's The Liquid Paper

It's the liquid paper. Many, many moons before the fish came the liquid paper. I became the liquid paper manager, delivering items of use to hundreds of agents citywide. As I moved over the years from one call center to the next, liquid paper became my staple.

Here is the story in a nutshell. One evening while managing a survey processing account, I was in need of motivation for my agents. My company wouldn't give me a budget to buy prizes, and that was a sore spot. Anything I wanted to do had to be done in-house, with my existing tools. Well, at first glance, one wonders what they have in-house to make things happen. Chairs, desks, file cabinets, telephones. None of that can be classified as prizes, unless one wants to take the risk of being arrested for theft. But my agents needed inspiration. The group had long faces and bored glazes in their eyes. We weren't making money. None of us.

I grabbed a key to the supply cabinet and ripped it open. I was looking for any prize that came in multiples. The liquid paper box was a natural. It came eight to ten in a box. I had my prizes. If my company wouldn't give me a budget to motivate their agents, then my company was going to get a purchase order for liquid paper supplies like they had never seen before.

Up and down the floor I went, hawking liquid paper like it was a million-dollar home. "Next completed survey gets your name in a hat for a chance to win this beautiful bottle of liquid paper," I shouted. Then, I got my team excited. "Look at this liquid paper. What a gem. Beautiful bottle, perfect for absolutely nothing. The round shape of the top tells you this bottle is an exquisite collectors' item, perfect for home and office use. Everyone here needs to qualify to win a bottle of liquid paper. Don't stop now. Next survey in the hour has their name in the drawing for a fantastic bottle of liquid paper."

I wasn't done yet.

"What does this liquid paper do, you might ask. Good question. It paints, its cleans, it smells the good smell many of you may remember from those high school days from long ago. The best part of liquid paper is that it's long lasting. It does your nails. It covers acne marks. It is perfect to erase mistakes caused by typewriters, laser printers, and pen marks. Best of all, it's non-toxic, low odor, nonflammable and contains no harmful solvents."

The whole floor was enjoying my presentation, and the goal had been established. Up and down the floor I went, showing off my bottle of liquid paper. Each agent absolutely enjoyed it. Some gave it a quick whiff. Others painted their nails. Others held on to it and rubbed it for good luck.

As the hour came to a close, surveys were being completed rapidly. 100% gain from last hour, 200% gain from last hour. The numbers were soaring.

Needless to say, everyone met their goal for the hour, and liquid paper became a favorite for the entire call center. Best of all, I got a budget from my boss and was able to buy multiple brands, colors and styles of liquid paper.

Throughout this book, we have touched upon some pillars of call center supervision that motivate performance and increase production. Pillars such as creativity, originality, service and performance on behalf of the supervisor take the basic business of managing a call center and step it up to a higher level. Your call center can be a Disneyland when you take a moment to think creatively about:

Desire + Concept + Initiative =Success

Desire + Concept + Initiative can work grandly for call center management, when management wants the call center to emphasize a philosophy that extends far beyond just a normal business department. I know there are hundreds of amusement parks all across the world, but I believe there is only one that captures the creativity, leadership and vision for its employees. That's Disneyland. When management wants to take fun ideas and transfer them to the call center, management and agents alike will believe that "*THEIR CALL CENTER CAN BE A DISNEYLAND*"

CHAPTER 13

Unique Ways To Motivate Call Center Agents And Open Communication

"There go my people. I must find out where they are going so I can lead them."
Alexandre Ledru-Rollin

• Have a team meeting and ask your agents for input about what they would like to see changed when it comes to the physical look of the call center. Take their suggestions, and make as many changes as possible.

• Prepare and distribute call center or team T-Shirts and have "T-Shirt Days" when the entire staff wears the same shirt for the day.

• Post large, poster-sized messages around the call center, thanking your agents for completing various tasks. Examples include:

"Thank you for working hard today"
"Thank you for showing up on time today"
"Thank you for doing what is best for the customer"
"Thank you for qualifying our clients correctly"
"Thank you for coming back from lunch on time"
"Thank you for doing a great job!"

• Produce a call center or department team newsletter on a regular basis. Include birthday news, longevity with company, personal news, product information, sales or customer service training, various happenings, quotes, pictures, etc. Let agents contribute articles, poems, and essays to the newsletter.

• Discover what type of simple food each agent enjoys eating. (Candy, Popcorn, Sodas, Mints, Crackers, Apples, Grapes, etc) Provide them with a personalized bowl at their desk, and keep that type of food in their bowl.

- Release a monthly cassette tape to the entire call center or department with some of the best calls recorded over the past month. Use these tapes for training and motivational purposes. Reward the agents who are on the tape with a special certificate or lunch.

- Provide each agent with a personalized engraved name plate. Include the company name or department name on the name plate as well.

- Set a goal for your agents and play the "ring my bell" game. Purchase a loud bell, or gong, and place it in a convenient location. Each time an agent meets their goal, they can ring the bell.

- Produce an annual department yearbook.

- Have a call center appreciation day, with continental breakfast, snacks, and various trinkets.

- Provide each employee with a budget for educational training. They can attend seminars or take community college courses. Also, provide agents with the resources to find training and educational events.

- Once a month, provide one lucky person with special recognition. Candy, flowers, extended lunch, leave early, and trinkets. Use the same date each month to condition your agents to expect the unexpected.

- Provide every agent with business cards, whether they use them often or not. Business cards can be a value-added perk that binds the employee to the company, and helps foster teamwork.

- Allow team leads that assist supervisors and managers to be elected and reelected every six months or every year.

- Have once-a-month roundtables with a different set of call center agents each month.

- Place an employee suggestion box in a convenient location, and print all employee suggestions in the newsletter.

- Allow agents to interview and participate in the decision-making process when hiring agents.

- Once a month, meet for lunch with your agents and ask them one question: "What would you do if you were supervising this department and team?"

- Allow each agent three extra hours every month to be creative, take time off and learn new skill sets.

- After an agent takes a special training class or educational seminar, have him prepare a fifteen minute short version, and allow him to present that version to your department or team.

- Use play money to motivate. Hand out play money for good deeds, and prepare a reimbursement system for prizes. For instance, $2000 in play money may equate to one extra hour of lunch, or a free call center or department T-Shirt.

  Have your team write a book, story or a song.

- Provide games and contests and award prizes. For example, a prize might be a free magazine subscription to the magazine of their choice.

- Once a month, have a "reward party" for a team member. That member must be nominated by his/her peers. Once a month, on the same date, throw the surprise party for the surprised winner.

- Put together a department talent show. Group agents into teams, and have them coordinate a show.

- Have your department or team write a book, a song, or a story. Each week, ask one agent to write from one line to a full page toward the book.

- Every morning, grab $1.00 in pennies or nickels (depending on the size of your call center) and walk around the call center handing change out to each person as a "motivational boost" to start the day.

- Buy breakfast foods and deliver them to the best performers from the previous day. Dress up in costume as a waiter or cook, and deliver the food using a push-wagon or a tray.

- Buy food for the entire group and serve breakfast to your agents.

- Invite three or four agents to coffee and donuts.

- Have team meetings away from the office. Use outside surroundings, such as a grass area or bleachers.

- Twice each week, distribute magazine articles that have little relevance to the direct job of selling over the telephone. For example, in the sales environment, hand out magazine articles that broaden your agents' abilities to sell their product. (essays, features, biographies, facts and figures, etc.)

- Write a personal note of congratulations to 3 or 4 agents and place it underneath their chair or computer keyboard.

- Call an agent into your office and chat with him about "nothing in particular"

- Use the internet to spur feedback and communication. Encourage your agents to read, and learn, by passing out a list of 2 or 3 web sites you feel would be beneficial to your agents.

- Randomly select an agent and send him an e-mail to promote conversation.

- Hide something of value in the call center, or in the department, and provide your agents with two or three clues to find it. (money, a gift certificate, etc)

- Have a day where agents switch seats with other agents and sell on behalf of their partners.

CHAPTER 14

Creating Employee Rooms And Organizational Teams

*"Give your agents the motivation
to succeed, and they will recognize the fact
that they must succeed."*

Dan Coen

Some customer contact centers go the extra step to build an environment that encourages agents to achieve. They take this extra step by taking the time to think out of the proverbial "box". (I'm certain you may have heard that old phrase used often: 90% of all management keep their thoughts and ideas in a box. To achieve success, think outside and beyond the box)

Employee Rooms

Below are some ways of getting the most out of your call center agents. By taking these examples and building on them for your call center, you will find that employees make the extra effort to come in even when they might not want to, think twice before choosing to leave their department, and perform better when they are at work because they are given the tools to do so. See if you can add any of these programs to your call center environment.

1. Call Center "A" has five separate offices that aren't used all of the time. They remain empty of people, but not of belongings, as much as 90% of the day. Certainly, not all companies have the resources of space to free up five full offices, but even finding a small amount of space is better than nothing. What should these recreational offices contain?

    a. The first space needed is an exercise gym, complete with a Stairmaster, a treadmill and a lifecycle. At any time throughout the day, an employee who is upset with a customer service call, or exhausted with any part of the call center world, can go into the exercise gym and burn off some energy. This area is a great stress reliever.

b.   The second area is a break room. Simple. Except this break room comes with a fully stocked refrigerator that stores all healthy foods, such as water, fruit and nutritional snacks. Within reason, any employee in the call center may help himself to refreshments, at any time. An optional donations jar is located in the room, as well. (Nobody may help himself to the donations jar, unfortunately!) This is strictly a food room, with couches and chairs throughout.

c.   The third area is a game room. In this room are games such as Monopoly, Checkers, Backgammon, Video Games and Cards. During breaks, lunch or stressed periods, agents may use this area in which to cool down.

d.   The fourth area is an unofficial training room. Not to be confused with the standard training room professional trainers may use, this room is designed for groups of agents to get together to learn new sales presentations, new product information, or any type of applicable residual training. Supervisors may use this "unofficial room" for quick training sessions. The room should be decorated with pictures and bookshelves should line the walls. This room is only to be used for call center related activities.

e.   The fifth area is the quiet room that mimics the fourth room. Lined with bookshelves, couches and pictures, the one difference is that this room is designed for agents who want to take a break or eat their lunch in solitude. This library is quiet, and the fact that nobody may speak makes it quiet. Not all the books are related to call center activities, and many are perfect reading for breaks and lunch and before and after shift times.

Certainly, not all of these rooms have to be utilized to create a powerful environment for your call center agents. One area is better than none, and it is clear that some areas may be combined. The message is clear, however. Give your agents the motivation to succeed, and they will recognize the fact that they must succeed.

Organizational Teams

I am a strong proponent of using organizational teams to make a call center department sparkle. I am certain you or peers of yours have been in situations where supervisors are responsible for performing every job themselves. Projects such as new employee training, residual training, product training, interviewing, company policy training, communications training, sales training, quick updates, intranet training, team meetings, etc. all fall to the supervisor. Not to mention all of the paperwork which accompanies each assignment. Even quality managers and supervisors can get worn down making certain that call center agents have everything they need to excel.

The question to ask yourself is: How can I better integrate the call center agents who want to be more involved in the department? How can I ensure that agents who wish to dedicate more time to important call center projects feel empowered to do so? The answer is often right in front of you. Below are fifteen team ideas that promote added performance and benefits in the call center environment. By putting these teams together and allowing employees to participate in the opportunities, the agents in your call center who desire to be more a part of the organization can get their wish. Best of all, your call center will benefit with many creative and influential ideas that you and your staff may not otherwise have developed themselves.

1. Manager Companion Team

The manager companion team provides an outlet for agents to volunteer their time away from the telephone. Management must make the decision to incorporate their agents into focus groups and to give them decision-making opportunities. For instance, one year I decided to have four manager companion teams. Each team would assemble for one quarter, and meet six times during the quarter. The team would be accountable for 1) providing communication about developments they feel should be brought to management's attention; 2) being a focus group for management and 3) providing an outlet for agents to achieve more in their call center.

2. New Product Distribution Team

If your business faces constant product changes, a product distribution team can help management facilitate transitions. Two or three agents are designated as "go-to-agents". When a new product is introduced, these agents develop the best way to communicate it over the telephone, create some quick bullet points, then create an introduction sheet and distribute it around the call center. Pre-technology days meant that every product folder in the call center must be updated by these two or three agents on the new product distribution team. With new technology, the intranet is a perfect resource. Agents still must go into the system to update the intranet, however.

3. New Hire Team

When it is time to interview perspective call center agents, use agents to facilitate the process. Agents do the job and they know what it takes to succeed. In addition, the ability to interview agents gives members of the new hire team some responsibility for crafting their culture and peer group.

4. Computer Training Team

In this age of new technology, a computer training team is invaluable to a call center. Why not have agents form the core of that team? If a staff of thirty agents uses the computer, invariably two or three agents each month will become rusty in various elements. A computer training team composed of agents helps ensure that all agents are able to utilize technology well. Remember, e-mail, voice mail, chat and transferring of telephone calls among peers must go smoothly to give the customer or prospect the best attention. Many times, peers in the call center complain that their teammates can't manipulate the computer well. This is their chance to rectify the situation.

5. Contest Team

Contests are designed for agents, so it's a fantastic idea to have agents help design the contests. In a typical customer contact center, supervisors develop contests and present them to agents. The goal is to keep agents motivated and energized to break records. Yet while the contests may be effective, my guess is that many of the more creative agents would relish the opportunity to build their own contests. Agents know what motivates agents.

6. Awards and Prizes Team

If your call center gives away the types of prizes they should, then your agents will find themselves motivated. Under the same premise as the Contest Team, your agents will find more unique prizes and awards that make a difference than supervisors ever will. I suggest you provide this team with two tenets. First, give this team a budget. Second, encourage this team to be creative. The *awards and prizes* team will bring some of the most creative awards to your customer contact center.

7. Sales Training Team

For those accounts that involve sales, I strongly encourage the development of a sales training team. I have heard too many times from supervisors that sales agents need training, and I hear that statement from supervisors who never utilize their top agents to assist in providing the training. Once a month, have the sales training team of agents put together real-life workshops based on their successes. Besides being effective, agents tend to believe that peers who do well know the secrets of their success.

8. Employee Monitoring Team

Monitoring checklists are valuable, and so is agent participation. Under the same premise as the *sales training team*, I have seen peer agents sit with individual agents who are struggling and turn them around. The premise that a peer agent is doing his own work and therefore can't hear what other agents are doing is a reality. That is a shame. Yet, sometimes agents do overhear other agents and provide impromptu training. This is good, although not structured. Under both premises, imagine a team dedicated strictly to helping their peers be successful, in a structured setting led by team supervisors. This works!

9. Company Policy Training Team

Obviously, human resources handles company policies. However, in the customer contact center, policies and procedures change all of the time. Management should gather together three or four agents (no more), who can take the changing policies of the call center and adapt them in an intranet format, or policy handbook, for the rest of the agents. In today's world, agents are confused all of the time by policies, and supervisors have little time to clarify. Let agents work for management!

10. Ideas Team

A general team to help management excel is needed. This team may assist with ideas on general structure, contests, prizes, motivation, training, etc. The ideas team does thinking when management is too busy to think. They may collaborate with all agents to bring pertinent ideas to supervisors.

11. Process Development Team

When new teams of processes are introduced, the concept is the easy part. The execution is difficult. I have found success inviting a process development team to help with implementation. How does a process get communicated to agents? How are processes developed for agents? A team can put it together much more fluidly than can a supervisor or two.

12. Birthday and Anniversary Team

This brings culture to the call center. It truly separates the run-of-the-mill call center from the world class call center. Everybody feels good when others remember their special days. Even though some won't admit it, it bring happiness to the work environment. When building call center culture, it doesn't hurt to make the work environment a little more like home.

13. Job Rotation Team

In today's world of changing dynamics, and changing employees, I encourage each agent to be cross-trained on all jobs. One period of time every few months can be the time when jobs are rotated. Besides building empathy in the customer contact center for the work others do, this makes each agent that much more valuable and experienced.

14. Competitor Information Team

In very competitive environments, the most effective companies know everything about their peers. The Internet has helped make finding competitor information easy. But who has the time? A team of agents dedicated to finding information, and presenting it via memos, fliers or the intranet, can turn your team of agents into a well oiled machine.

15. Educational Opportunity Team

This team both presents educational programs for their peers and also finds educational opportunities for agents. Clearly, learning opportunities are very valuable. Six or seven agents looking for classes have a better chance of finding those learning opportunities than does one supervisor.

Supervisors will not always be responsible for managing each team. It is the top agents who should oversee the teams. For instance, the Process Development Team may consist of three members who meet once a month and discuss potential processes. The team leader may be a veteran agent who sets up meeting times and dates, takes notes, assists in putting together proposals, etc.

How can management form teams in the call center?

1. Management must identify why they feel a team is necessary and what goals that team should attempt to accomplish.

2. Teams must have very motivated leaders.

3. The team leader should send out a memo explaining which teams are being formed and what their initial objectives are.

4. The team leader should ask agents to "sign up" next to the two or three teams they wish to be a part of, and have them return the form to the team leader's office by a certain date.

5. The team leader should place agents on appropriate teams, ensure

that there is a mix of senior and new agents, and, ensure that every team has enough strength to sustain it. "Strength" in this case is defined as agents who will participate. The worst thing is to have a team dissolve because none of the participants play.

6. Do not have more than three or four agents to a team.

7. Set the meeting time and dates the first time around, and appoint a captain of each team at the meeting dates. Make sure everyone recognizes the importance of carrying out their duties.

8. Develop a brief synopsis of goals and objectives for each team. At the first meeting, identify what needs to change in the synopsis, and what will work.

9. Give each team an assignment and a date when the assignment is due.

10. Make sure that the agents recognize how valuable the team leader feels their participation is to the performance of the call center Re inforce this from time to time.

CHAPTER 15

The Heart Of A Call Center: Contests, Prizes and Awards

*"You can't depend on your eyes when
your imagination is out of focus."*
Mark Twain

The best part of a day in the life of a call center manager or agent exists when prizes and awards are introduced to motivate performance. When prizes and awards exist, management and agent get energized passionately in a way one would rarely expect. Properly placed prizes and awards change the tone of a call center world dramatically. Whether your call center focuses on member services, sales, or some other goal, some of the contests, prizes and awards I will list in the following pages can help turn your center into a department that breaks records.

Prizes and awards give a call center flavor. Agents tend to have trouble staying on the telephone, much less being spectacular on the telephone, and they relish the chance to be rewarded when they go above and beyond the call of duty. Prizes and awards not only provide that recognition, but they give management opportunities to influence agents, motivate performance and compel success when management needs to do just that. Prizes and awards help provide a reason for management and agent to do something successfully.

I am certain that many readers have seen or heard about call centers which use awards and prizes effectively. Perhaps you have been excited about making an impact in your own center using prizes and awards. Maybe you haven't introduced prizes and awards because you have been so busy with other duties. Or maybe the company budget is stopping you from introducing prizes and awards that make a difference. Or perhaps you have prizes and awards in your call center, but you feel they aren't improving performance dramatically enough. My objective with this section is to see that you, your call center and your agents come out of that slumber and make a concerted effort to introduce prizes and awards that help you find success.

I can't emphasize enough how motivated and focused agents become when properly placed prizes and awards are introduced into the call center. Here is an example of how prizes and awards can condition behavior. I remember the time I worked in a call center that gave away $100 cash at the end of each day. While I am solidly against giving away cash prizes, particularly of that amount, I watched closely how the $100 conditioned agents to react and communicate and take direction from management in a way that they never would have acted without the $100 bounty. At the end of the day, when the agents crowded around to see who would be the lucky winner of the day, there was a flavor to the call center that no other business, or company department, could emulate. One hundred dollars is quite a bit of money, and that one prize changed the direction and communication of our call center immeasurably.

Before we review the litany of prizes and awards that I feel work best, I'd like to take a step back and first provide a foundation with regard to how call center management should plan for developing prizes and awards. It isn't enough for management to believe that any prize or any award will condition behavior and provide flavor in the call center. Management has to recognize some of the ground rules that help to make prizes and awards successful events.

1. Pick a theme around which to base the awards

The best prizes and awards are those that have a theme to them. Themes may include:

Entertainment

Sports

Fantasy

Adventure

Animals and People

Your Product or Service

An end goal

By introducing a theme to the call center, agents and supervision better focus themselves on creating a consistent atmosphere. I have been a part of call centers that gave out random prizes and awards month after month, and I noted that there was no overriding "concept" to the program. Agents and supervision never could put their finger on the theory of prizes and awards and how to make them valuable to a call center, and because of this I felt impact was lacking. On the other hand, I have been an intricate part of many call centers that based their prizes and awards around certain themes, and I have seen these programs make a world of difference. The one difference that stands out is that throughout the year, agents and supervisors came up with one creative idea after another to build on the theme of the call center. Therefore, although the theme may have been developed and introduced in one month, the true potential of that theme wasn't realized until the entire staff had a chance to provide their input. As the months wear on, the greatness of a theme is exposed.

As an example of a strong theme, many call centers have a sports theme. Their teams have sports names and their call center is decorated with posters, balloons, and sports paraphernalia. Prizes and awards are centered around sporting goods certificates, food certificates to sports restaurants, sports clothing, sporting event tickets, and the like. Themes are usually six months or one year events. For example, one year you may decide to have "Sports World" in your call center, and the next year you might move to "Amusement Park World". Large corporations that provide general prizes and awards for all employees usually have some sort of promotional event in place. In that case, perhaps the call center will build on the theme that the company as a whole deploys. Therefore, if the large company as a whole has "Animal Prizes and Awards" as a theme, then the call center will build on that theme in one fashion or another.

2. Make it a point of consistently budgeting for awards, and consistently presenting awards

Without a clear budget, prizes and awards always disappear just when agents need them most. Even when a budget is in place, be certain it's written in stone. For example, if management is given $150 every month to use for motivational purposes, management will probably plan the next few months using that budget. If all of sudden they find the money has disappeared, an entire call center can go into a graveyard spiral. I have produced prizes and awards on a monthly budget of $10, and on a monthly budget of $2500.00. Price doesn't matter. Consistency and buy-in from finance and upper management does matter. When presenting awards, do so in consistent meetings. Perhaps the senior manager meets once a month with the entire customer contact center. At that time, awards are presented. Agents must be conditioned to expect certain functions will take place.

3. Allow many categories of agents to receive awards

Don't only recognize your best agents. Don't only have one or two categories that are considered "best" categories. I once had five categories that I distributed prizes for, which was fine. Unfortunately, I left out one very critical category which I also should have given prizes for. From then on, I have made it a point of thinking long and hard about what categories I wanted to present prizes and awards for, and then made sure I was rewarding the right number of agents for their accomplishments. One category I always try to include now for any prizes and awards involves a subjective category. That way, I can use my own judgement to reward someone who may not know he was even being considered for an award.

4. Deliver awards utilizing a positive presentation

If you have a consistent event where you hand out all the prizes, or even if you inconsistently hand out prizes to agents, make sure your presentation builds on the excitement of the prizes and awards you will be handing out. A presentation to an agent should be a celebration of that agent's success, not withstanding the number of times that agent has received a prize or award. The supervisor should be clear how valued the agent is for achieving the prize or award. The entire department should be able to see the value in the prize and award, and understand they should attempt to do everything they can to earn one for themselves. In fact, management often makes the error of forgetting to reward an agent by mentioning to that agent and the entire department how many times they have achieved success. In presentations, be certain to know how many times a particular agent has qualified for prizes and awards, what the feat means in the big picture of the entire call center, and how you appreciate that success. If Agent "W" has qualified for a particular trophy four times in the last year, be cognizant of that number and let the other agents realize how successful Agent "W" is.

5. Give awards for both the biggest, and littlest, reasons

Prizes and awards don't have to be for the grandest categories. As little a feat as showing up to work on time for one month may be worthy of a prize in your call center. Management makes the error of trying to inspire only the top categories of performance, and management fails to realize that even the smallest categories are of importance and worthy of recognition. Certainly, a top agent should be given an award for having the most talk time in the course of a definitive period, such as a week or month. In addition, a top agent should be given an award for working on a special project one time, whether that project only took five minutes or one day to complete. Recognition matters!

6. All good deeds are not worthy of awards / Any good deed is worthy of awards

Two agents may do the same thing in the call center, but only one agent may receive an award for it. Why? Let's take a drastic example to explain a simple point. If one person can't walk and one person can, would you give an award to both people if they both take small baby steps? Absolutely not. The person who couldn't walk but manages to take small baby steps deserves an award much more than the person who can walk and has taken small baby steps his entire life. This allows the supervisor to use awards for the right reasons and to motivate and inspire everyone, when applicable. I like using the "most improved agent" award to show that some good deeds should be recognized. If agents see that one award is presented for most improved, then perhaps they will try to earn the award the next time.

7. Change categories on a regular basis

The key to quality prizes and awards are that the same categories are not utilized all of the time. Management needs to assess categories based on the requirements of the call center. Management should not be afraid to change categories in order to keep agents striving and active for success.

8. Don't let a lack of budget affect your agents' aspirations

The number one reason management doesn't provide prizes and awards in the call center is because they don't have a budget to do so. Most call centers do not have a budget for prizes and awards. When there is money to spend, they spend; when there isn't, they don't. Obviously, developing a budget for prizes and awards isn't a simple process, but even a small budget of $10 every month is more than enough to provide prizes and awards that your call center agents will value. Price is no object when management needs to motivate and recognize. Many of the items I list below can be created with little or no money.

In many large corporations, senior leadership fails to understand why they need to budget for awards, contests and prizes. A misguided philosophy of "we're paying them, that's all they need" is pathetic. In effect, games are the hidden foundation to successful call centers. They help demonstrate to the agents that the company has an investment in their success.

Some of the simplest and best prizes and awards in the call center

Gift Certificate To Anywhere
Restaurant Gift Certificate
Movie Gift Certificate
Sporting Event Tickets
Music Paraphernalia
Shopping Spree Tokens
99 Cent Store trinkets
In-House Gifts

Amusement Park Tickets

Lottery Tickets

Playing Cards

Spare Change

Little Notes and Messages Providing a prize or award

Home Movies

You

One hour extra lunch, paid. (Manager sits for agent)

Liquid Paper, Paper Clips, Rubber Bands, Binder Paper

Magazines and Newspapers

Magazine and newspaper subscriptions

Food from the candy machine

Time Off Work

Manager Sells For You

Gift Baskets

Sales and Communication Books

Cassette tapes and CD's for learning opportunities

Fiction and Non-Fiction Books

Automotive Repair

Send a letter home to their family

Picture Day. Take an instant picture

Stuffed Animals

Seat Cushions

Key Chains With Their Name on it

Hotel Accommodations for one or two nights

Trophies

Balloons

Posters of favorite Celebrities

Baseball, basketball or football signed by management

Team or department shirts, sweaters, jackets, jerseys

Contests

The art of contests is not simple. The wrong ones will not motivate your team of agents, and in fact it may de-motivate them. A poor contest provides them with no inspiration, and makes them wonder how focused their management team is on them. In addition, contests have a life of their own, and not all contests have the same lifeline. For instance, the contests with exceptional prizes and a quick start and end date are contests that provide bang. But, multiple ones back to back tend to fail. On the other hand, long contests for months or a year lose momentum as personnel change and objectives are forgotten, sometimes making those a waste of time.

Every call center has a different program, product and service, so management must base their contests around what they need. I have seen call centers with one-year-long contests followed by twelve monthly contests, and I have seen call centers with fifty-two contests. Some of them worked and some failed. Those that worked started with management's commitment to make the contest. Management had a foundation and a program to make it happen.

The key to orchestrating positive contests is to develop both the contest and the promotional material to impel agents to relish the contest. Most supervisors develop a quality contest and introduce it with little fanfare or follow-up to ensure the contest is achieving desired results. The second step of this two-prong attack is as critical as the first. Marketing and promotion of a contest keep the momentum moving. Fliers, e-mails, voice mails, memos, signs, art work, awards, displays, parties, meetings, etc. all help take a contest from introduction through conclusion. The public relations of a contest excite agents and keep energy high. Treat the promotion of a contest quite the same way that marketing departments treat the promotion of a product or service. Be creative!

Below are some general techniques all supervisors must recognize when building contests in their customer contact center:

1. Most prizes and awards should be presented to agents because of a contest or event

Make sure your contests lead to awards, and your awards center upon some sort of contests. You can run contests for one hour or one year. The one hour contests should be utilized for quick boosts of activity, but they also wear down quickly. Agents like the one hour contests for a few hours, but need a break after awhile. Yet, if you forget to introduce prizes and awards, the contests become meaningless.

2. Competition makes people excel

The supervisor who feels that his agents don't need or want contests is missing the boat. In any customer contact center, the ability to generate competition exists. Management can harness that ability into programs that lend results.

3. Contests are driven by prizes and awards first, the actual contest second

This is a basic principle of call center supervision. A terrible contest can be a great success if a world class prize awaits the winner. A world class contest can be a bomb if the prize is pathetic. The end result for competing provides agents with as much, if not more joy, than the rules of competition. Make your awards valuable!

4. Never run a contest longer than a month

Although this can be disputed based upon your call center, I have found that the longer a contest runs, the more likely the contest loses steam. If management does run a contest longer than a month, then management better have promotional marketing programs designed to keep the focus and commitment of agents. Without a strong public relations campaign, the contest will be stagnant. Remember, turnover is a hot topic in call centers. If your call center has turnover, how many agents will be eligible to "win" a six-month contest? If new agents come into the call center, how do they qualify to "win" a contest already in progress? With exceptions, I like to keep contests in the four to five week range.

5. Never make your contests confusing

I have designed so many confusing contests that the only person who thought it would do good things was me! If contests are going to be motivational, they need to be simple and specific. Their job is to impel agents to do better. The last thing you want agents to do is get confused about a contest designed to make them perform better.

6. Never make your contests disruptive

The contest should be an addendum to the daily job, not override the daily job. You have a poorly developed contest if it causes arguments and battles between agents vying for the opportunity to win. If agents spend more time analyzing the contest than doing the work to make the contest succeed, then the contest is complicated and overly ambitious.

7. Make certain the manager always has the final decision

When you create a contest, be certain you display a "start date" and "end date" to the contest so the agents recognize exactly when it starts and finishes. In addition, put in writing how results are determined, and who is responsible for final judgements. Trust me. Agents will find loopholes if you do not find them first.

8. More than one person may win

If a contest only has one winner, then a contest is only geared to a handful of folks. I like tiered contests that provide a multiple number of awards for a multiple number of winners. In a customer contact center of one hundred agents, perhaps twenty to twenty-five can win a contest. The 25th place prize may be a pencil or pad of paper, but, as I've stated in previous chapters, those are some of the best prizes.

9. Never give away money

Once you give away cash, you devalue all other prizes. Even though every prize is bought by a cash transaction, the direct prize of money makes all other prizes seem useless.

10. Create contests using widgets and percentages and measurements

Contests that involve an element of competition tend to work best. However, widgets involve exact goals and exact numbers. If you want an agent to make seventy-five sales in a month to qualify, then the number seventy-five must be attained. Percentages can give agents a first-place win without having to achieve the exact goals that management needs. In a paltry month, an agent may earn 35% of all sales, tops on the team. Prizes are awarded to this top agent. Yet, nobody, including this agent, may have met the objectives. Based on a curve, this agent was victorious. However, it is questionable where the call center benefited from the contest. Therefore, most sales environments tend to do better when widgets are the measurement of choice.

11. Always have concrete and clear goals

Don't waver on your contests. No exceptions. No confusing end-results.

12. Don't over-contest the department (Don't spoil them)

My biggest concern with contests are that they won't achieve desired results. Even the best contests will not get valuable results if agents are literally exhausted from trying to meet contest goals.

13. Make the contest winners feel special

The more special they feel, the more likely the next contest will be a grand success.

Exciting Contest Ideas For Your Customer Contact Center

It's The Plasticware

Meet your goals and get some of the cheapest off-brands made. A Plasticware set for $3.00 can have as many as five or six pieces. A supervisor can give those away one at a time or as a set. Agents love the concept because it is so silly. Plus, they use the Plasticware at their desks to house plants, candy, money, paperwork, etc.

It's Free Food Friday

It is hard to get workers in on Fridays. Make Friday the most fun day of the week, and provide free food to entice them. Build a contest around the week leading up to Friday. When your call center becomes the most popular place on Friday night, then you have true success.

Star Game

Every call center must have a star game. Put large charts on the walls with team members' names on them, and each day the agents meet their goals they get a star next to their names. At the end of the contest, every star equals a prize. In a fourteen day contest, the maximum attainable stars is fourteen. Give prizes for stars. Don't hesitate to provide bonus stars for special events, too.

"The Partner" Game

Not all agents enjoy playing this game, but it builds teamwork in the customer contact center. For a period of time, say two weeks, agents switch seats and work for other agents. Perhaps each day at 3:00pm, the switch takes place.

One Hour Off Game (Manager works)

One hour off work game is a great contest. It's better when the manager sits at the seat and works for the agent. This builds teamwork among all factions of the call center, as agents see their supervisor doing their job. Most importantly, agents who get one hour off work value that opportunity.

Grab Bag Game

A large grab bag with one hundred or more simple giveaway items goes very far. Any game or contest can be developed around the grab bag. Perhaps the agent who gets the most sales in an hour period, or the best average answer time in a day gets to pull one or more prizes from the grab bag. By going to the ninety-nine cents only store and spending one hundreds dollars, you can fill a grab bag fairly easily.

Team Competition Game

Any contest that involves teams generates a strong level of excitement that contests involving individuals don't generate. Teams may be of any size. A team contest may incorporate fifty teams of three agents each, or ten teams of fifteen agents each. Don't be shy about building creative team ideas, and promoting end results around teamwork.

Quality Checklist Game

Some of the best contests revolve around quality checklists. When agents understand that prizes are based on performance using the telephone or computer, agents do everything they can to excel. By itself, a positive score means nothing more than personal satisfaction to the agent. However, when prizes are awarded for those with scores in the ninety percent range, agents have added motivation to perform admirably.

Free Food Game

Many of my contests in the call center involve food. Food motivates. Perhaps an end result prize for meeting goals may be an ice cream social, or a catered lunch, etc.

Buddy - Buddy Game

Similar to the team concept, I am a strong believer in playing buddy-buddy contests. If the goal for each agent is fifty sales, then a team of two must make one hundred sales. Even if one agent performed eighty percent of that number, both parties contributed to the victory, so both win prizes.

The "Medals" Program

Because contests and prizes revolve around visual rewards, medals are a natural progression. Think of ways you can introduce two to four categories of medals in your daily call center. Gold, Silver and Bronze is one option. Blue, Red and Green is another. Any themes can be used. The enormous pride that agents have when winning medals is demonstrated when they hang the medals at their desks, or show them off to friends and family. Medals also supply a motivational reason for those who didn't win a medal to strive to win one for themselves.

Hot Potato Game

This is a truly fun contest. As a football moves around the call center, the supervisor decides when the football stops. At that point, the person holding the ball has a chance to win prizes by meeting that day's objectives.

The Personal Goal Game

Very simple. Give each agent a personal goal for the day, week or month. Write the goal on a piece of paper, and make sure the agent buys in to that goal. It must be reasonable and achievable. Work with each agent to measure progress. Although each agent has a personal goal, few agents write that goal on paper and stay focused on that goal throughout the month. A contest helps agents to focus on their goals.

CHAPTER 16

Career Pathing

"Since every agent is at a different stage in his/her professional development, the development program is set up as an ongoing process, each step being initiated by the individual."
Dan Coen

In each facet of organizational development, the opportunity to advance within a company is a prime motivator for employees. It builds stability into an organization and encourages commitment. One example of this is the way the various branches of the military are organized. The armed forces in this country have developed their program of advancement remarkably well, and this has reaped benefits throughout the years. From one level to the next, military personnel understand that clear objectives must be met in order to gain promotion. In the call center environment, because call center supervisors spend time training agents and rewarding them for achievement on the telephone, agents often understand the basic measurements needed to earn promotion to the supervisor / team lead level. (i.e. be a top agent on the telephone, show up all of the time, develop strong communication skills). Yet, they sometimes see advancement as an arbitrary reward based on too few outlined objectives. Agents anxious for opportunities regularly exclaim "Why am I not getting promoted? How come there is no training so I can move to the next level?"

Considering that implementing a quality agent development program will be advantageous for call centers long term, I find it surprising that most managers fail to do so. This is especially mystifying since so many call centers today are adding clients and increasing call volume at record levels. By not focusing on agent development, call centers enhance the risk that their employees will take the skill sets they have learned and go to work for competitors across the street! This leads to a question call center managers should think about more often: ***How can managers pave the way for their agents to grow within the organization?*** In response to this question I have developed a precise formula for training and promoting call center agents to the next level. Its objectives are two-fold. First, to establish a career-path opportunity within the company so agents will recognize and value the opportunities. Second, to increase the skill level of agents so that their contributions to their departments, and the company, reach the highest levels possible.

Develop a Complete Agent Development Program

In my program, all agents who choose to do so are immediately enrolled in a development program from the first day on the job. Since every agent is at a different stage in his/her professional development, and some agents may be pleased with their present positions and not looking toward promotion, the development program is set up as an ongoing process, each step being initiated by the individual. The agent is expected to complete every level at his/her own pace. Agents are not eligible for promotion until they complete all steps. This program encompasses the following four levels:

1. <u>Understand The Supervisor Level Throughout The Organization</u>

Before agents in a company progress to the supervisor level, they need to recognize that their linear job of utilizing the telephone is going to disappear, and the larger role of managing a complete operation will become a priority. This means they are going to have to regularly interact with other departments. We all know agents who say "I don't know why supervisors in this company are making those decisions, don't they understand?" Clearly, the agent hasn't taken the initiative to find out why supervisors are motivated to make the choices they make. Moving from agent to supervisor requires the individual to be cognizant of performing within the established corporate culture, and to develop arenas in which he/she can affect corporate culture for the better. To assist each agent in understanding the supervisor level, I ask each agent who participates to visit three departments from a list I provide, and to meet only with supervisor-level employees from those areas.* I want the agents to find out exactly what the supervisors in those departments do on a daily basis, how they interact with our department, where they find their greatest challenges in succeeding, and what they think makes a strong supervisor. I want them to see how management functions on an individual basis and as a group. Following the meetings, I request that the agent prepare a paper on his/her findings, with a slant toward the topic <u>How Other Supervisors Interact With Call Center Operations.</u>

*   *(See below for a list of departments that I provide to my supervisors)*

2. Develop Exceptional Communication Skill Sets

Agents who have an opportunity to become supervisors usually have above-average communication skills. But will they be able to communicate with their peer agents, supervisors, and upper level management with the same effectiveness? To determine this, I want agents to focus on a few critical elements of communication to see if they recognize this problem along with other dilemmas. The first assignment involves delivering information. I intentionally give each agent in training an opportunity to deliver written and verbal information that I might have delivered to various departments and staff. They may be communicating with call center agents, senior staff or supervisors. My objective isn't to see how the message is received, but rather to see in how organized and consistent a manner the message is relayed. For instance, the message "Dan wants us to staff X project this way" should come out "To achieve our goals, we've confirmed that we need to staff X project this way".

The second communication assignment involves having the agent secure buy-in with our direct staff. Because I believe buy-in from all staff is critical for call centers to succeed, I work hands-on with the agent on some of the skills I feel work best in gathering buy-in. This includes polling for ideas prior to an announcement, asking for consensus, listening for feedback and adapting policy if necessary.

A third communication assignment encourages agents to explain their thoughts to me in written format about their concept of team-building and motivation. This tests their creativity to explain how they recognize employee development in the call center. I may pose questions such as "If we had to design a new team structure for our entire department, how would you go about planning it?" or "What five motivational tidbits do you find most effective when trying to motivate your level (agent) in doing their day-to-day jobs?"

3. Conceptualize The Call Center And its Possibilities

Through this development program — and independent of it — I would like to see all elements of staff create new opportunities in the call center. Conceptualizing what the call center isn't is much more important than seeing if the agent recognizes what the call center is. I am always encouraging agents to come to me with ideas about how to create better programs for success in the call center. Supervisors are very often responsible for creating or maintaining a culture among their employees which demands success. My overriding message is for the agent to create something new. Perhaps it is a new statistical tracking process, or a new policies and procedures handbook. Oftentimes it may be a new team structure or motivational contest. Perhaps the agent proposes new forms of communication, such as the regular use of e-mail or fliers or overhead projectors. Or maybe the agent is responsible for formulating a "Bill of Rights," or "Standard Principles" document that will pace the organization through a difficult challenge. Creative imagination is important for any supervisor position. So is the ability to develop programs independently.

Conceptualizing the call center should be an intimate examination as well. It's sometimes unfair to have agents judge their peers, but it can be enlightening too! Let's face it, an agent today may be managing his peer tomorrow. For some agents, it is nearly impossible to grade, praise, or criticize a peer. This inability is one of the primary reasons why many call center supervisors are hired from outside the company, and not through the agent ranks. Many agents simply can't adjust to managing friends, and those friends oftentimes have difficulty respecting and following their former peers. I sit with the supervisor candidate and I learn all of his/her thoughts regarding the agents he/she may manage. I ask questions such as "What are their strengths?" "What do you see in them that would make them strong supervisors?" "What areas do you think you can help them with?" I insist that the agent and I develop action plans with regard to how they would go about training their agents should they have the opportunity. These case studies are invaluable. We work on mock reviews of agents. Of course, this process wouldn't be relevant if I didn't have the agent perform a mock review with feedback on my skills as well!

4. Perform Specific Assignments

The final step in my development program consists of the assignment of special projects to the agent. A large part of managing a call center involves consistently creating programs that will make the call center function better. For instance, I may suggest that an agent change the daily management routine of a small department. The objective is for the agent to perform research on possible new routines, ask questions of peers and upper management to see if it is practical, review budgets if applicable, and produce a "white paper" of the new management structure for that department. Another project may involve meeting with peers from other companies and touring call centers. I am a firm believer that call center tours are one of the most valuable ways to increase the skill level of one's own call center personnel. These tours can be set up so that the agents visit various call center conferences around the country, or similar companies in the area. Very often, companies will agree to reciprocate, choosing to visit your call center in return. The knowledge the agent candidate gains in reviewing other practices is invaluable.

Conclusion

Prior to promoting any agent, managers must be certain that the agent has the ability and prerequisites to accomplish the job by meeting the above criteria. It is incumbent upon the manager to ensure that a comprehensive training program is initiated. This will provide agents with the opportunity to grow and will guarantee motivated and long- term employees.

FOUR TESTS TO DETERMINE IF AN AGENT IS CAPABLE OF BEING PROMOTED TO A MANAGERIAL POSITION

1. Is the agent candidate capable of maintaining accountability for multiple projects, departments and programs? In other words, can he/she be accountable for results, staffing, supervisor responsibilities and sustaining the structure of operations?

2. Does the agent candidate possess an exceptional understanding of practical call center applications? This includes understanding the concept of technology and how it can play a role for supervisors and agents; grasping the purpose of statistical evaluation to judge performance; recognizing the impact of other departments that directly interact; and identifying what motivates the call center to function each day.

3. Is the agent capable of managing agents in a way that encourages a positive and successful call center culture? This would gauge whether the agent is able to grasp the big picture of management. Some agents thrive as leaders of a team, but fail when they lead the large entity because they fail to understand the elements that go into a call center culture.

4. Can the agent communicate information to employees, peers and superiors in a way that motivates them to move forward? Communication is the force that drives supervisors and agents. This means the supervisor must determine what communication needs to be delivered, and how it needs to be delivered, in order to ensure that operations are consistent.

* <u>Choose three departments from the following list:</u>

Human Resources, Technical Support, Customer Service or Inside Sales (when applicable), Field Agents or Outside Sales (when applicable), Quality Assurance, Account Management and Finance.

CHAPTER 17

Why Supervisors Forget New Agents

"Supervisors are so obsessed with meeting core goals and objectives, and adapting to requirements and requests throughout the day, that they very often forget to provide new agents with the detailed, hands-on training that new agents must have to break records."

Dan Coen

I have noticed that after new agents get smothered with supervisor attention over their first five or ten working days, they often have the misfortune of becoming all but forgotten. One can call this the *"build them up and ship them out"* mentality of managing. Supervisors provide the training, show the agent the ropes, and say *"Good luck, let me know if you need anything."* Supervisors are so obsessed with meeting core goals and objectives, and adapting to requirements and requests throughout the day, that they very often forget to provide new agents with the detailed, hands-on training that new agents must have to break records. Of course, the irony is palatable at best. Supervisors need their agents to break records, yet they can't focus on all of their agents all of the time, and they lose track of focusing on new agents. Then, when new agents fail to break records, supervisors see a problem developing. They sit down with those new agents and orchestrate a performance development plan to help them get up to speed before being forced to take real action. But supervisors have the tendency to do these performance development plans <u>after</u> new agents have demonstrated they are not meeting minimum objectives, not before, when new agents need the training most. Many times, agents are silently crying out for more training and attention throughout their first weeks and months but don't get it. At the same time, supervisors are crying out for new agents to pick up the techniques to excel and break records. Somehow, the fantastic initial new agent training that the supervisor began in earnest becomes a trickle of training at best.

Let's look at nine reasons why supervisors fail to provide continuous training for new agents, and some solutions for each:

- <u>Supervisors are so busy working with veteran agents that they do not have the time to spend with new agents</u>

Veterans produce 90-95% of what a supervisor needs, so it is only natural that the supervisor will work with veteran agents first, in order to ensure that all company and departmental goals are met. More importantly, there is only one supervisor per X amount of agents. When in initial training, the supervisor is focused on his new group. Once the new group reaches the call center floor, they blend in with the other agents, and no longer stand out as they once did.

Solution: When new agents begin a job on the telephone, keep them all in one central location. If, for instance, three new agents start on Monday, make sure all three sit next to one another in the same area of the floor. This will allow the supervisor to have easy access to all three agents when one has a question or when the supervisor chooses to do initial training with the new agents. In addition, the three new agents will have created a bond with one another through their mutual relationship as new hires; therefore, new agents have the chemistry to ask one another questions and solve problems that may have not been addressed in new hire training, and to form a unit of motivation to keep one another striving to meet and exceed their goals.

- ### Supervisors tend to forget new agents exist because they are new and quiet

  New agents are sensitive to "getting along" with their supervisors. Therefore, when they have issues and concerns, they will either keep those issues to themselves or find a peer to assist them. The supervisor is generally the last person who is contacted on everyday questions a new agent might have.

  Solution: Meet with new agents each day for three to five minutes. Ask questions, search for opportunities to coach, encourage feedback. Ensure that the new agents feel confident they can come to management without losing their supervisor's confidence in them. Design a residual training program that covers one or more topics each day in those three to five minutes.

- ### New agents are fundamentally intimidated. They are shy

  They want to do the right thing, and they recognize everything they do may be the wrong thing. They don't know the ins-and-outs of the company, so they are more likely to suffer for long stretches with a problem than to ask for assistance.

Solution: New agents stay to themselves because they haven't developed a comfort level with their direct supervisor. Yet, they may do many things that they aren't sure about. Pair each new agent with a veteran agent. Allow the veteran agent flexibility in doing his job while assisting the new agent in learning the ropes. Many new agents would rather ask what they consider to be a "silly question" to a fellow agent, than to their supervisor.

- **New agents haven't yet learned the fundamentals of the call center culture, so they are unsure of how to ask for assistance**

   They don't know what is going on. Although they hear their peers talk and see their supervisor interact, they are still leery as to what is happening, because they don't have the experience in this call center to recognize what is new and what is a regular call center occurrence.

Solution: Continually encourage open feedback. Ask questions of your new agents. Promote acceptance when they ask you questions. Use silly rewards such as candy, lottery tickets and free lunch coupons to motivate new agents to ask questions.

- **New agents don't excel in sales or member service immediately in relation to their peers, so they don't stand out and make themselves visible**

   There is less of a visible reason to communicate with them or congratulate them for their performance.

Solution: Management must find reasons to cheer their agents on. Making one sale each day for a week may be worthy of prizes, even if the sales goal for each day is four or five sales. Management must see their new agents in a different light. Everything a new agent does well should be reinforced to that new agent.

- **Supervisors expect new agents to be quiet and unassuming as they learn their jobs**

   Therefore, supervisors don't expect to hear from agents on a regular basis.

Solution: Require new agents to ask one question a day of management. Support those questions with a reward process.

- **Supervisors are focused on other happenings in the call center, and don't budget their time accordingly to work with new agents**

Solution: Put yourself in an agent's role. They need help to succeed. They want help so they won't fail.

- **Supervisors obtain more enjoyment from working with veteran agents than they do working with new agents, because veteran agents bring supervisors their success**

Solution: Veteran agents leave the fold at one point or another. Top supervisors must continually "recruit" new agents to take their places.

- **Supervisors would rather see new agents sink or swim on their own, and supervisors don't want to put in the requisite time to assist them to swim!**

Remember that the new agent is probably the least valued and most critical figure to a successful call center. Without new agents, call centers would cease to exist.

Solution: While a supervisor has many duties to perform, the supervisor must take a moment to remember that he placed the new agent in his position. Therefore, he must have recognized the agents potential. Time management is key. Most supervisors find it is easier to spend the first or last part of each day with the new agents.

CHAPTER 18

Assimilating New Agents To A Veteran Team

"It is so tiring managing those needy, needy people
that suck the life out of you every day"
Anonymous

When it comes to assimilating new agents to an existing team, it is safe to assume that call center supervisors will almost always face the same challenges that our school teachers face. Or, more tellingly, new agents entering a new work environment almost always face the same challenges that new students entering a new school environment face. <u>Managing call center agents can be as vexing as managing elementary school students</u>.

We have explored in a different section the relationship and analogy between call centers and schools. Let's explore that relationship a bit more closely as it relates to assimilating new agents into a veteran team. I can recall two or three situations when I was a new student entering a foreign environment full of veteran students. New school, new classmates, new teachers, new expectations, new results. All the students knew one another. They had established relationships and rapport. They were formed into cliques. They recognized how the system of that school worked. They knew the key players. They could get results. I can remember feeling afraid, not for my safety, but for my future. I remember wondering if I was going to be able to assimilate into a new community, and accumulate the friends and relationships I needed to become successful. New students walking into a new school for the first time, staffed with veteran students, feel confused. The school is a modicum of practicality and routine. The new student is the X factor.

New call center agents are encumbered with the X factor, too. From a supervisor's perspective, observe how difficult it is for new agents to enter such a relationship-driven environment as the call center world. Agents are the new kids on the block, entering a set routine, with veteran agents already established. It can be incredibly difficult for professionals of all levels to endure. Agents have established their cliques, and they know how to get results. In the working world, results can mean money, promotion, opportunity, and excitement.

New agents expect from their supervisors a basic level of assistance when it comes to assimilating them to the veteran team. They also expect veteran team members to assist them in learning the ropes. Most veteran team members will help, but not all. For example, in the sales environment, it could be detrimental for one agent to help another agent to learn the ropes, for they may be competitors as well as teammates.

Supervisors owe their new agents an opportunity. I have seen supervisors preclude their new team members from any opportunity because they don't provide their new team members with the tools to succeed. Veteran agents sometimes are the easier clique to manage, so supervisors tend to take the easy road and foster success from their veteran group rather than working to achieve success with their new group. Here are a few steps call center supervisors must take to ensure their new agents become acclimated to their new environment.

1. Pair each new agent with a veteran agent.
2. Encourage new agents to monitor veteran agents before starting their jobs, and periodically during the shift.
3. Stay away from the new agent in the beginning so they can find comfort without being concerned about their supervisor's responses.
4. Provide feedback and monitoring updates frequently.
5. Teach presentation stances.
6. Keep new agents positive.
7. Explain failure.
8. Don't assume the new agent knows what you know.
9. Appoint veteran agents as team captains.

CHAPTER 19

Recognizing how new agents view technology

"The more opinions you have, the less you see"
Wim Wenders

All call center managers will agree that the challenges of new-hire training are daunting. New agents see dozens of faces, become acclimated into a fresh company structure, learn a unique program, and are trained on strange computer equipment. They are asked to understand the culture of the organization, and to immerse themselves in the daily gossip and routines of the office, as they get to know others in the office and choose new friends. A new agent must learn the policies and procedures of his company, grapple with sales and communications training pertinent to the program, and become comfortable with the work hours of the job. It all can be very challenging, and if the agent fails to execute even one or two aspects of the job extremely well, the agent will be set back in his objective to earn money and find success and comfort long term.

Recently, a new challenge has developed for agents going through initial training. The Internet, Intranet and web-based enhancements have joined CTI and CRM to turn the call center into a dynamite technology-oriented environment. The way telesales agents sell and the way customer service agents manage client expectations has been renovated because of their ability to make calls faster, take calls more quickly, manage processes more smoothly, and understand circumstances more clearly. Because the agents interact continually with computers, dialing systems, and ever-improving technology, agents now begin their first days on the job more concerned about the technological requirements of the position, and less focused on the communication and product aspects of the position. The first questions out of an agent's mouth generally are "How do I use the computer? What type of computer programs will we use? Am I required to learn a dialing system or database programs? Can you tell me about the technology and how to use it?" I estimate that 85% of my new hires have been intimidated by the computer and various aspects of technology both before and during their first weeks on the job. In my opinion, this is damaging to their initial training.

Managers must be cognizant that mastering technology should be an agent's *least concern*. When management begins to look at technology as the medium that motivates and supervises employees, then management begins to allow technology to take over a people-oriented job. Leadership, motivation, coaching, supervision, growth, structure and opportunity are people jobs that technology can support, but not replicate. Instead, agents should focus on the core aspects of the job that they will be performing day-in and day-out. Some of the aspects of the job warranting particular emphasis are:

1. Has the agent learned the characteristics of the product?
2. Is the agent ready to successfully communicate with customers and sell the product over the telephone?
3. Does the agent have the potential to become a well-rounded, positive employee?
4. Will the agent contribute to the well-being and success of the call center or department?
5. Does the agent understand the standards he is expected to meet?

To achieve successful training of new hires, managers should be sure to emphasize the importance of everything in the call center environment that is *not* related to technology. Technology has been perceived to be the savior for call center management, and in this perception management has taken a wrong turn. Technology is an addendum to the management of a call center. Technology is a support mechanism for supervisors and agents. But technology cannot replace quality management. Technology cannot replace the all important people factor. For instance, management should spend their initial training time providing instructions on how to be an enthusiastic team player and individual performer in the call center and on the telephone, long before they address the technology issues. In the sales and customer service environments, this includes meeting and exceeding minimum production goals, improving on ways to sell and communicate programs, adding considerably to the culture of the call center through ideas and actions, establishing dynamite relationships with peers, and assisting the department and company in attaining core objectives through excellent work habits and accountable performance. I believe that new agents will eventually learn the technology surrounding computer systems as time goes on. It may take two days or two months, but by the sheer nature and requirements of their positions, agents will become proficient, if not expert, at utilizing the various predictive dialers, ACD set-ups, and computer databases. The error in new hire training is that agents often spend so much time enamored with perfecting their use of technology that they fail to grasp the real skills that will lead to success in the field.

When I present a new training program, I first explore extensively the challenges of technology, because I want new agents to recognize their own thought patterns and fears. I encourage them not to be afraid of technology, because technology exists to assist agents in their daily jobs. I remind them that technology is a learned skill and reiterate that if management wanted technically proficient artists, they would have hired from the IT or MIS departments. I stress that agents have the tendency to panic over the challenges of technology, thereby failing to learn the programs at hand. After I have explained the technological basics to my agents, and provided them with a reference manual regarding these tools, I then advise them to concentrate on the other, more important aspects of the job.

All managers should spend some time, on the first day of training, reviewing and summarizing the technology to be used in the call center environment. To fail to do so is to leave agents in a state of paralysis. However, managers must always remember to never lose sight of the skills that actually lead to success on the telephone. Use your technology. Cultivate your human capital. Human Capital is the reason call center agents have been hired in the first place.

CHAPTER 20

Call Center Agents In the New Technology World

"Changes in the call center occur every year, and the technology being invented today is redefining management along with management measurements."
Dan Coen

The new world of internet connections, e-mail communication, instant chatting amongst parties, and 24 /7 information has changed the skill sets for agents in the call center. In the past, agents had to have decent computer skills. Today, agents must be able to effectively manipulate a multitude of separate instruments, such as telephones, computers, ACD, predictive dialing machines, and the internet. Computer skills have become a necessity.

I maintain that the key to new agent success is the work on the telephone, not away from the telephone. In telesales, if an agent can sell on the telephone, that agent will learn, through necessity, to use the technology around him. Hiring agents first begins with finding employees who have the capability of making money for your business by communicating exceptionally well on the telephone with prospects or customers. I joke that, as long as an inside sales agent can make money on the telephone, the supervisor will sit right next to him and "input" all of the sales. Yet, in the new world of technology, talking or selling well via the telephone is not enough to succeed. Other skill sets are required for agents to enjoy success. Changes in the call center occur every year, and the technology being invented today is redefining management along with management measurements. In essence, call center agents must take a leap forward in five critical venues.

1. Agents must be able to learn new systems. In the coming years, doing things the same way simply will fail. If a corporation institutes an intranet option, agents must embrace the option to better themselves, their company and their peers. Most notably, an intranet option can benefit the prospect or customer.

2. Agents must be willing to be flexible to handle upgrades and changes.

In the foreseeable future, upgrades and changes will be the mode of execution for customer contact centers. Management will continually upgrade their systems to meet new technology, and to adapt their call center to the internet.

3. Agents must conceptualize the advantages that modern technology brings to their job. The performance level that agents meet today is catapulted in great part by technology. So is their income level. Agents need to recognize that the most difficult upgrades and computer enhancements will become the most beneficial to their job performance.

4. Agents must embrace the internet, intranet, and e-mail, and instant messaging. They must relish in new web-based applications. The telephone will always be a major component of most customer contact centers. Even internet companies, which are predicated on web chat, e-mail and instant messaging, use the telephone for customer interactions on a regular basis. Yet, agents will be required to use multiple forms of contact opportunities to perform their jobs well. If today, your call center is 100% telephone based, perhaps tomorrow it will be segmented into four or six different channels.

5. Agents must get away from "the paper thing". The intranet replaces the unwieldy binders that store product information. E-mail takes the place of memos. The computer allows agents to store e-mail and intranet information in easy-to-access folders.

CHAPTER 21

Creating The Supervisor's Job Description

"The ways in which supervisors communicate policies and rules determine how effective those policies and rules are to the culture of the call center."
Dan Coen

Call Center supervisors are the backbone to operations and performance. Supervisors, the management line that directly manages agents, direct the culture and performance of your business. Why? Because they lead and motivate the front line agents. They inspire agents to break records. They manage people, emotions, statistics, results. They train agents in all facets of call center operations, from sales and communication training to company policies and procedures, computer and technical training, and product training. I analogize supervisors as double patties in a Big Mac sandwich. There are layers above the supervisor and layers below the supervisor, just as there are layers above and below the double patties in a Big Mac. Those layers above and below the double patties rely on the patties to provide answers to how good the sandwich will taste. Those layers above and below the supervisor level rely on the supervisors to provide answers as to how well the call center functions. Both the layers below and above the patties succeed or fail based in great part on the ability of the patties to provide a punch. Supervisors are the patties that provide the punch. They set the table for agent success or failure. If you are a team leader, consider a name change. You are a patty!

Your agents will perform well because your supervisors will inspire them to perform well. Senior management that forgets this basic tenet probably will not have a call center worth bragging about. When monitoring sessions need to be completed, it is the front line supervisor who completes the assignment. Agents unhappy with their jobs, or their performance, will complain to their supervisor, who carries the message to senior management. Supervisors have to roll up their sleeves and handle disciplinary actions, terminations and promotions. While senior management creates policies and rules, supervisors decipher those policies and rules so the agents can understand them. The ways in which supervisors communicate policies and rules determine how effective those policies and rules are to the culture of the call center. World-Class supervisors who understand culture and the balance of culture within their call center can put out fires before they escalate into department-stopping dilemmas. Emotions can be manipulated by top supervisors who understand human nature, and the emotional influence of human nature over call center agents. Senior management may take credit for agent performance, but while agents should receive nearly all the credit for their performance, supervisors deserve accolades for keeping their agents focused, energized and prepared. Supervisors teach agents how to sell; they instruct agents to communicate better to customers and prospects; they serve as a sounding board to agents when the agents need a wall off of which to bounce ideas and frustrations.

Supervisor Job Description

I would venture to say that a large number of call center supervisors fail to understand their daily and weekly job duties. They perform each day without any thought as to what their jobs really entail. In many call centers, it is the supervisor who receives the fewest number of training hours. He may receive some element of product training, some computer training, and maybe some training on interacting with other departments, such as human resources or technical support. But from that point on, development is minimized and practical application of the job is accelerated. Call center supervisors are asked to perform with little foundation. As one boss said "Throw them out into the fire, let's see what they can do!"

Yet, in order for supervisors to make a strong impact on their agents, they must understand the principles and requirements of their jobs. What is a supervisor responsible for? When does the supervisor's role become his boss' role and not the supervisor's responsibility any longer? What steps must a supervisor take to manage, motivate and ensure that agents are exceeding performance standards? While putting together a job description sounds like a basic task, it breeds complications. Most supervisors do not have a clear-cut guide as to what they should do on a daily basis. Even fewer supervisors have beacons to guide them in their relationships with their agents. Yet, the core foundation of any call center is built upon the supervisor's job performance.

For an example, analyze athletics. In athletics, one finds only a few coaches who take the time to develop and implement outlines as well as detail job duties for each player. Coincidentally, it is those coaches and those teams who win championships the majority of the time. Coaches who get terminated because their teams do not play well are usually criticized by their players for not explaining to each team member his unique role and objectives. Players on losing teams routinely make comments such as "I didn't know when I was going to play, so I was never ready." Or "One minute they want me posting up and scoring, the next minute they want me slashing to the basket." Or "It was never made clear what my duties were." No matter how skilled coaches are, they must communicate to their players succinctly the exact role and responsibility of each player.

One example of a winning team can be found in professional basketball. The Chicago Bulls won six world championships in the 1990's. Their coach, Phil Jackson, spent years in the minor leagues formulating his winning strategies, and then took those strategies with him to the Bulls. The concept of roles and responsibilities was merely one of the many concepts he identified. Foremost to this basic concept was the theory that each player must have a role.

Supervisors who understand their role in the call center can direct the call center to success.

On those Bulls teams, Michael Jordan knew that he was the key go-to player and the scorer on the club, and his teammates understood Jordan's role as well. Scottie Pippen, one of the top 50 basketball players of all time, recognized that he was not the number one option — Jordan was — but Pippen recognized that he was the next player in line, and he was prepared to perform should Jordan falter. Dennis Rodman knew he was a defensive specialist and a rebounder. He was not to score. Ron Harper and John Paxson, both traditional scoring guards, understood that they were a complementary guard team to Jordan. As a distributor of the ball, they supported Jordan, and also would score when Jordan or Pippen were not available. Forward Toni Kukoc, a superstar player his entire career in Europe, became an off-the-bench star, subbing on behalf of the starters. His job was to provide scoring, defensive pressure, ball handling and passing skills when applicable. Shooting guard Steve Kerr had only one assignment as a player on this team: to shoot 3 point baskets. For Pippen, Rodman, Harper, Paxson, Kukoc and Kerr, their roles were defined by their leader, and they worked fluidly within that system. Each player understood his assignment. From day one, there was no confusion. The result was an NBA dynasty. (In the 1999-2000 season, Jackson's first in Los Angeles, he coached the Los Angeles Lakers to an NBA championship. The team's recognition of "roles" played a large part in their growth from playoff contender to world champion)

Transfer basketball to the call center. It does not matter how small or large your call center is, or how many agents your supervisor may manage. Your supervisor's job is as important to your agent's performance as Phil

Jackson's job was to his players. Jackson understood this philosophy, and he brought that knowledge to his players. Your supervisors will affect the performance and opportunities of each call center agent as often as the head coach of an NBA basketball team will affect the performance of his players. That most important step begins with defining roles. Can each supervisor in your call center say, unequivocally, day-in and day-out, that he knows his roles and can build on his roles to help his agents break records in the call center? If not, then it is your agents who will suffer.

Sample Supervisor Job Description

Below is a sample supervisor's job description. I encourage you to amend this description to fit your specific customer contact center.

Supervisor's Role:

The role of a call center supervisor is to educate, motivate and support *your* team of call center agents. This is established through hands-on management, continuous agent training and accountable leadership. *The supervisor is in a service-oriented position within the call center.* For instance, on my honeymoon in Hawaii, I was struck by how complementary the entire staff of our hotel was. "Mr. Coen, do you need this? Mr. Coen, may I get you that? Mr. Coen, what can I do to make your stay better? Mr. Coen, if there is anything you need, don't hesitate to contact us." It wasn't until I got back to my job as a call center manager that I recognized that *I am the service person, and my agents are the guests.* I found myself saying the exact same things to my agents as were said to me when I was a guest in the hotel. "Larry, may I get you anything to make your job easier? Marcia, how is your day going today? Vince, what can I do to make your sales go more smoothly? Manny, if there is anything I can do for you, don't hesitate to come see me." Put simply, the supervisor's role is to serve customers, and his customers are his agents. When the supervisor begins to serve interests other than his agents', his effectiveness will be dissipated.

I teach that supervisors must practice a program I call "memorable touches". A "memorable touch" involves the supervisor making the effort to go to each of his agents many times throughout a shift for the simple goal of providing a "memorable touch". This is the ultimate service approach. By asking if the customer needs anything more, and whether the customer is enjoying his experience, waitresses provide "memorable touches" to their patrons. A call center supervisor can practice "memorable touches" by presenting a similar experience. These touches include a simple "hello", an empathetic conversation about performance, a review of a past conversation, a motivational tidbit, a positive comment, etc. The job of a supervisor is to provide as many "memorable touches" as applicable to each agent, in order to ensure each agent feels motivated to continue to thrive. A "memorable touch" does not only involve talking directly to the agent. It can involve writing notes, leaving e-mails, recording voice mails, printing fliers, or copying sales or product articles.

Supervisor's Responsibilities:

❏ Manage a team of call center agents.

❏ Be available to affect the entirety of the team's operations.

- ♦ Manage by walking around. Be visible to answer questions.
- ♦ Take calls that your agents can't handle and be available when an agent appears to need assistance.
- ♦ Monitor queue and track inbound calls. Keep agents <u>aware</u> of inbound calls, calls waiting, abandonment rate, etc.
- ♦ Motivate and encourage agents through positive communication and feedback.

Being available to affect the entirety of the team's operations differentiates a supervisor from senior management. To effectively build call center culture, the supervisor is responsible for "on-the-floor" activities, and must be available to assist agents while agents are "on-the-floor". Senior management has a role that involves less floor time. When call centers take supervisors away from the main floor for meetings, they are affecting time the supervisor can use to motivate his agents. The supervisor should spend the entire call center shift on the floor. (*Conceptually*, most managers understand this. On a *practical* basis, supervisors find themselves off the main floor, and in meetings, as much as 80% of their time!)

❏ Meet at least once each week with your team. At a minimum, review the following topics:

- ♦ Review the past week's events, including statistics, results and industry news.
- ♦ Disseminate new product information to the agents.
- ♦ Discuss a sales theme or point-of-interest topic for the agents.
- ♦ Introduce new staff members.
- ♦ Present commendations and awards.
- ♦ Communicate company information.
- ♦ Answer questions and comments.
- ♦ Provide agents with a glimpse of future weeks.

❏ Perform at least one monitoring evaluation with each agent every two weeks
- ◆ Spend 30 minutes to one hour monitoring the agent.
- ◆ Spend 20 to 30 minutes reviewing the agent's performance with the agent. Use a formal monitoring checklist.
- ◆ At the conclusion, copy the checklist and put it in the agent's file
- ◆ Give the original checklist to the agent.

❏ Keep track of attendance, daily statistics, paid time off, sick time, etc.

- ◆ Ensure administrative bookkeeping is accurate.
- ◆ Create and maintain files on each agent as they relate to attendance, production, and reviews.

❏ Present to the Project Manager at the conclusion of each week a breakdown of the _past week's_ monitoring checklists and a written performance summary of the team.

❏ Present to the Project Manager at end of each week a breakdown of the _next_ week's monitoring assignments and a plan for the team.

- ◆ Create a forecast describing the things each agent will be focused upon.
- ◆ Create a detailed plan of the way in which you plan to impact your team's day-by-day performance
- ◆ Divide the team into three groups. (top, middle and bottom)

❏ At the end of each working day, take three minutes to log into the "daily notebook" any feedback, analysis or reflections from that day's interaction with the agents.

❏ Recruit new staff and schedule existing staff to meet service level objectives.

- ◆ Interview and hire staff. Assess needs / plan ahead.
- ◆ Develop schedules with agents each month to ensure call center objectives are covered.
- ◆ Schedule residual training, departmental meetings, sales training, and computer training.

❏ Spend four hours per month working the call center telephones.

- ◆ Make sure your staff recognizes that you can do their jobs, too!
- ◆ Truly understand what your call center agents are facing.

❏ Administer training programs for new hires and existing staff.

♦ Work with management on refining and scheduling appropriate training sessions.
♦ Develop training documents that support call center operations.
♦ Create residual training pieces to foster growth.

❏ Develop contests, awards and themes that increase agents' loyalty and focus.
❏ Produce a quarterly "white paper" outlining your team's performance and growth. Paper should be no more than three pages long. Topics to explore include:
❏ Team performance for three month period.
❏ Individual performance of core, focus and new staff.
❏ Team and Individual analysis of upcoming quarter.
❏ Supervisor disappointments of past quarter.
❏ Supervisor successes of past quarter.
❏ Notable team and department information.
❏ Establish monthly meetings with other departments to review call center operations.

♦ Meet with human resources to review staffing levels and employee issues.
♦ Meet with peer staff to coordinate new hire, residual, product, computer and sales training.
♦ Meet with MIS to review computer hardware, software and database issues.
♦ Meet with outside field staff to review upcoming events and call center / outside participation.

❏ Produce performance reviews as established by Project Manager.
❏ Create effective channels of agent feedback.

Characteristics Of A Top-Level Supervisor

❏ Understands the supervisor's role within the call center.
❏ Focuses on his/her team and people first.
❏ Creates a supporting and consistent culture.
❏ Recognizes how the team, and project, functions within an organization.
❏ Conceptualizes and establishes a proactive planning process each day.
❏ Motivates, Teaches and Learns how to be a better team leader.
❏ Understands technology.

- ❑ Uses company statistics to gain maximum performance from individuals.
- ❑ Communicates and Listens.
- ❑ Thinks creatively.
- ❑ Sustains positive energy.
- ❑ Manages by walking around.

What makes a poor call center supervisor?

- ❑ No interest in creating relationships.
- ❑ No interest in building and sustaining relationships.
- ❑ Apathetic with regard to the job.
- ❑ Lazy with regard to the job.
- ❑ Unmotivated to create a positive environment.
- ❑ Does not handle change well.
- ❑ Complains Constantly.
- ❑ Is impatient with the agents.
- ❑ Is bored with the job.
- ❑ No desire to coach or teach.
- ❑ Causes disruption among peer ranks.
- ❑ Doesn't use technology to better operations.

Poor supervisors don't understand the essence of people— management. They don't have a desire to build a strong communication culture. They have no interest in seeing the call center through their agents' eyes. They have little recognition of how strong a factor emotions play in dictating performance. They don't understand the value of creating feedback and communication opportunities. They don't see the call center as a creative opportunity.

What to look for in hiring top supervisors:

1. A supervisor must see the call center as a place of creativity.
2. A supervisor must understand the value of incentives, awards, and contests.
3. A supervisor must <u>want</u> to be accountable for his team's performance.
4. A supervisor must understand how valuable communications and feedback are to call center performance.
5. A supervisor must see his team of agents as a participatory element to the entire organization.
6. A supervisor must desire opportunities to advance and improve the call center.
7. A supervisor must be able to demonstrate patience and master his emotions.
8. A supervisor must be willing to coach, train, create and innovate.

9. A supervisor cannot be afraid to practice *desire + concept + initiative.*

10. A supervisor must value the importance of motivating his team. He must be able to understand <u>how</u> to motivate agents.

11. A supervisor must practice C.A.L.M.

Managing Through C.A.L.M.

A supervisor's management style must rely upon structure. Call center supervisors cannot supervise themselves and their agents, strictly based upon whims and reactive actions. Every great supervisor has an understanding of why they are great, and why their agents respond to their platform. This structure underscores their abilities to supervise creatively. It ensures they get the most from their employees. As my first few years of supervising employees trickled by, I narrowed my management philosophy into four simple themes. I call these principles C.A.L.M., because the acronym C.A.L.M. represents the main goal of supervision. No matter what happens in the call center, nor how often agents push a supervisor's button, the supervisor must remain C.A.L.M. to achieve maximum performance from his agents. C.A.L.M. involves patience and understanding. Some questions I pondered over the years while I refined this philosophy included:

♦ What do agents need most from their supervisors?
♦ Why are some supervisors better performers at providing agents what they need?
♦ What supervisor traits assist agents to break records?
♦ What supervisor techniques must be practiced daily in the call center?
♦ How does the relationship between agent and supervisor thrive?
♦ Why is a supervisor given certain responsibilities, and not others?

C.A.L.M. has guided me in my everyday dealings with agents, peers and upper management. It strengthened my recognition of how to act and what <u>not</u> to do in situations that warranted expertise. Supervisors must take time to think inwardly about how they want to manage their agents. Thinking inwardly means identifying their core management constitution. Are they slave drivers or hands-off supervisors? Do they manage by walking around, or by sitting in place? Do they counsel or criticize? Do they motivate through actions, words, or a combination of both? Do they allow agents to prepare for what is coming each day, or do they keep agents on their toes? Do they think of themselves before, or after, their agents? In call center management, there is a great difference between "experience" and "expertise". Experience encompasses nothing more than years doing a job. Expertise involves learning while doing a job, and becoming an expert at it. Call Center supervisors with fifteen years experience but no overriding management philosophy may lack the talent and skill sets that a supervisor with four years of expertise has. C.A.L.M. are four overriding philosophies that help turn experienced supervisors into expert supervisors.

Consistency:

When one supervisor says *heads* and his counterpart doing the exact same job at the exact same time says *tails*, the call center has a problem. Two supervisors managing 10 agents each must supervise those agents with a basic consistency. If a call center has no pattern that agents can grasp onto, the call center has a culture issue. Consistency is the thread that ensures a call center is run correctly. "Is management doing the same thing, the same way, each time? Are call center agents responding to this consistency?" Call center supervisors must manage with a mode of consistency. Examples include:

a. Start the day.

b. Greet agents exuberantly.

c. Conduct meetings.

d. Expect agents to bring items to your plate.

e. Demand that objectives are met.

f. Manage the day in segments.

g. Resolve conflicts as they arise.

h. Train employees.

i. Report to management.

j. Motivate agents.

k. Motivate staff.

l. Develop contests.

m. Think of future challenges.

n. End the day.

The main guideline in managing supervisors and agents is this: they can't perform for you if you confuse them with inconsistent expectation levels. Would your staff perform better or worse if you were eternally inconsistent? Worse, of course. Would you perform better or worse if you were eternally inconsistent? Worse, of course. Does performing successfully once and changing your habits the next day breed success? (An example of the importance of being consistent can be found in athletics. Would a good coach urge his team to practice one way, but play another?) The call center environment is no different. Supervisors must do the same thing, the same way, each time.

Accountability:

Is management held responsible for their supervisors? Is management held responsible for their agents? Should they be? Does anybody care about what is done each day? Who should care? Accountability is the cornerstone of a call center operation. I have walked into call centers that have little supervisor accountability, and I have been mortified by what I've seen. Agents realize that when supervisors are not accountable, supervisors won't stop agents from doing what they want to do. I have seen call centers flounder due to a lack of accountability. No matter how much money is spent creating first-rate technology, supervisors must make it a point of trying to be accountable for the success or failure of those under them. In a customer service or sales environment, supervisors must know what their agents are doing. They must set valid limits, and enforce those limits. Great supervisors can bring world-class accountability to a call center and affect their agents by taking the following steps and grasping them as reality:

1. Establish urgency and direction. Enforce urgency and direction.
2. Select agents based on skills, merits and abilities. Make agents accountable to earn selections.
3. Pay attention to the information disseminated in meetings and communications. Implement that information.
4. Set clear rules of behavior.
5. Challenge agents with fresh facts and ideas.
6. Present positive feedback, rewards and learning opportunities.
7. Pay attention to responsibilities.

Leadership:

Any book on management will have detailed descriptions about leadership. Is management full of managers or thinkers? Leaders or followers? Creators or debaters? In the call center, the actions to be taken for good leadership are very cut and dry. Supervisors are leaders. They point agents in a direction that agents must thrive to reach. Therefore, as leaders, supervisors must have basic essential leadership qualities. Examples include:

1. Supervisors must present reasons for agents to excel.
2. Supervisors must want to create opportunities for agents to excel.
3. Supervisors must be able to take initiative on their own, without guidance from management.
4. Agents must feel a sense of guidance from their supervisors.
5. Supervisors must disseminate product information in an easy-to-follow formula so agents may use it to their advantage.

6. Supervisors must be more than caretakers. They must be teachers and coaches.

7. Supervisors must be passionate about opportunities. Passion is expressed via motivation and energy.

Motivation:

Is there an understanding about what needs to be done to keep supervisors and agents performing at peak levels? The best supervisors have a good understanding of what motivates agents in the call center. If the boss of XYZ department in a business walked in and handed each employee a bag of candy from the supermarket, the employees would be thankful, but the gift wouldn't promote extra performance from those employees. In the call center environment, a bag of candy from the grocery store is worth 2-4 weeks of first-rate telephone performance. To truly get under the psyche of agents and bring them to a level of motivation that impact results, a supervisor must do a bit of the following:

♦ Analyze each day as a new beginning and decide what you need to do to motivate the agents.

♦ Be funny with your agents.

♦ Utilize your hearing skills to understand exactly what each agent is trying to articulate.

♦ Plan events to keep your agents selling.

♦ Perform offbeat functions that maintain levity and performance.

CHAPTER 22

Building Retention and Performance Through Successful Compensation Agreements

"A compensation plan is not only a set of numbers that determine pay. It is an emotional pact between management and agent that shapes a culture."

Dan Coen

Instituting a new compensation agreement is one of the great emotional challenges for call center management. It's like playing with matches, lighter fluid, and gasoline in a forest of trees. The wrong agreement can destroy an entire call center culture. The wrong plan usually leads to another wrong plan, which leads to another plan. In a matter of weeks or months, the revolving plans take any steam right out of the job. Agents become distrustful. They don't have the passion they once had for the job. They simply lose their focus. Management must create a new compensation plan once, and it must be very good; one that can last for the short term, and for the long term. Management must make a strong effort to consider the emotions of their agents in creating the new agreement. A compensation plan is not only a set of numbers that determine pay. It is an emotional pact between management and agent that shapes a culture, identifies the values of a corporation, builds relationships, and constructs the foundation for the future success of the call center.

Perhaps management forgets that they need to develop a compensation plan that works for the call center while also creating a plan that works for the agents. Management may understand they need to look out for their agents. But realistically, they are in management to incorporate the best plan as a whole, and agents can very often come out on the short end of the stick. On the other hand, agents see one point of view regarding compensation plans - theirs! Yet management has a multitude of scenarios they must take into account. If the compensation plan doesn't motivate agents to do well, the company suffers and the plan becomes an albatross. The entire environment becomes one of complaints, bickering, and attrition. Emotions rage because management has tinkered with the agents' most prized possession. If the compensation plan compensates agents too well, the company can also suffer, and the plan becomes an "agent vs. management" issue. All of a sudden, management is paying above budget for performance, and bottom lines become affected. Management then takes steps to correct their first error, and raging emotions become prevalent again.

Creating a new compensation agreement involves creating change. From one plan to the next, agents must change their mindset and personal goals to meet new objectives. Because change is considered by many to be unfriendly anyhow, change involving the way one gets paid accentuates agents' concerns. If the compensation plan penalizes agents in comparison to what they had before, they feel this is retribution, and turmoil ensues. They want to know why the plan has penalized them. They want to know why they should continue to perform at the same level, or even a higher level, when they are being paid less. They want to know how management developed this new plan, and during what timeline management may change it again. The truth is that management almost never changes compensation plans to give their agents more money. They may change a plan because goals have changed. Or they may change a plan to reduce the level of income attainable. But agents and management recognize that changing compensation plans always has some sort of "dent" involved. It may be a change in policy or a change in payment, or a reduction in money or a change in payable terms, etc. When management makes changes, it is nearly always not to the benefit of their agents.

Can management recognize that designing a new compensation plan involves playing with emotions and playing with change? I implore them to recognize that they must. Emotions and change are two combustible elements that may skyrocket, or destroy, performance and retention. Emotions and change that impact money only add fuel to the fire. How many times has an exit interview turned up the themes of money, emotions and change as reasons for leaving? How many of those people have also gone through one or more compensation agreement changes over the past year of employment? The concept of making more money is always at the forefront of an agent's wish list. Yet, most agents do not get upset when a compensation plan does not allow them to make more and more money. They understand that corporations have budgets. They want steady raises for steady performance. They want to be paid well for performing well. But they never expect swings in money to outweigh reality. Agents simply want money not to be taken away. They don't want to be treated below par for performing the same way they did yesterday. They don't want to learn that management must pay agents less for the same work. They don't want management to pay them less while also asking them to perform well. Call Centers suffer when agents feel their chance to make the same money they presently make is being manipulated. This change in compensation elicits wild emotions. Of course, this may be said about many industries. Professional athletes perform excellently in order to be paid handsomely. Would they perform excellently if each year they were provided less and less? Sales agents attempt to excel consistently in order to achieve bonuses. Would they excel consistently if their bonuses were reduced for the same work? The list can go on and on. Nothing is more important to the agent than making good money for good work. One of the quickest way to lose quality agents to the competition is to forget that agents always want to be rewarded fairly for excellent performance. Changing compensation agreements can change the way agents perceive they are being treated.

When new compensation agreements are introduced, neither emotions, change nor money are usually discussed with any depth. Sure, management knows pay is changing because they have the calculator out and they do the math. But how many times does a management team leader talk to his staff about emotions, change and money while they sit in a conference room and design a new plan?

Instead, a change in measurements is what gets the most attention. If the change in measurements clearly is one that the agents feel negatively impacts them, then agents begin asking questions to themselves and their supervisor. Why are you not paying us for something you used to pay us for? Why are you paying us for areas that are out of our control? Why are you changing the requirements for pay? Why do you feel a need to change measurements?

Creating a compensation plan

When I develop compensation agreements for telesales and customer service contact centers, I begin the process by framing the issues for management. The first issue I frame, as I touched upon above, is that management must decide why they are changing the agreement. Is it an economic reason, such as does management want to save money? Is it a measurement reason, such as does management need to pay based on different measurements? Is it a company strategic issue? Once we decide on the answer, I make sure that management looks at every alternative and objective prior to changing compensation plans. Does management realize the emotional toll of introducing a new agreement? Does management understand that those agents they don't want to penalize often are the agents who get penalized? For instance, if management wants to change the plan because of a change in budget, management must figure out who gets hurt most by a change. Usually it is the high performers and key assets to the organization who suffer the most penalties. The agents who have done exceptionally well at performing at the level they were asked to perform at are the ones who suffer. I have been in rooms when senior management has said "Let's not change our low-end people, because they aren't costing us anything". (Whose end are you changing then?) If management is changing a compensation agreement to meet new measurements, I always insist that management take time identifying what they want out of their measurements first. Then comes what they want out of their compensation plans. Why? Because compensation plans are always based on measurements. Management says "Let's pay them X amount of dollars for eighty sales instead of sixty sales." The compensation of X is a direct correlation of the measurement of eighty instead of sixty. If eighty was not the appropriate number, say seventy should be, then the measurements are off. And if the measurements are off, then compensation will surely not meet expected objectives. Measurements that change need to be rock solid, or compensation will not accurately follow.

Once we have taken our time framing the important concepts, I assess the following sixteen segments of a call center's business prior to changing a compensation plan:

1. Budget
2. Ability to Pay
3. Base Salary Possibilities
4. Hourly Salary Possibilities
5. Commission Possibilities
6. Bonus Possibilities
7. Career Path opportunities within the company
8. Environment of company in relation to competition
9. Culture of call center in relation to competition
10. Budget in relation to competition
11. Goals and objectives for the call center and for the agent
12. Project scope and responsibilities
13. Revenue versus non-revenue generating positions
14. Management support
15. History of compensation plans
16. Future Business Plan. 6 months, 1.5 years, 3 years, 5 years

My objective is to learn what the call center has at its disposal. For instance, not all call centers can provide answers with regard to each of these sixteen segments. To design a plan, management must know all its options. Some of the above steps may not be currently a part of the call center, but can be. Other steps may have been analyzed and discarded.

Once an assessment has been completed, I take seven principles and I apply those principles to the above sixteen segments. These principles are my guiding philosophies when designing compensation plans. Every time I present my findings, I support them by using these seven principles as the foundation.

1. The compensation plan must be centered around a company's ability to pay

Every company is different when delegating a certain percentage of pay to its agents. Management must be cognizant of how much money and investment the company can make in the call center. Traditionally, outbound telesales agents always earn more commission than inbound customer service agents, because it is believed that outbound telesales agents have the more difficult job of creating new business. But have you noticed that, more and more, member service and retention has played a larger part in growing businesses? Once a finite portion of the market has been reached in a sales campaign, the battle for business comes from achieving winback sales from competition, not creating new sales. Therefore, the ability to retain a member through member service retention and customer service soft selling can become more valuable to a firm than generating new sales. Businesses are beginning to spend a high percentage of their resources on maintaining client relationships so competitors can't steal their clients away. In many industries, maintaining relationships with current clients is more profitable than farming for new business. Therefore, I ask the question: "Where does a business want to spend its money? Why? What exactly is a firm's ability to pay?"

2. The compensation plan must be centered upon demand

Developing a compensation plan in the heart of a large city is quite different from coordinating a plan in the middle of a small town. Simply put, part-time agents located in small college towns demand a different pay scale than full time employees in major cities. What is the demand in your city for call center agents? In addition, demand applies to more than the battle between part-time and full-time agents. There is internal demand as well. As a call center executive, I have seen top employees transfer to other departments, depleting my staff. We were never disappointed if the agent left for better career opportunities. We were always disappointed when they left to work in a department that paid more, even when we felt the value of their work in that department paled in relationship to the value of their work in our department. My philosophy has always been that it is better to overpay an employee a little than to lose an employee of value because you paid too little. When designing a plan, ask about the demand within the company for quality employees. Observe the demand within your industry. Weigh whether it is valid to pay a little too much, or a little under par, for your agents.

3. The compensation plan must be centered upon job requirements

The job duties for agents are completely different from project to project. No two call center jobs are the same. Some duties involve answering incoming e-mails, others involve making outgoing telesales calls. Just because an agent has "XYZ" job duties in one call center or in one project does not mean his job duties will be exactly the same on a different project or in a different call center. A compensation plan must be centered on the objectives of each particular job. Requirements to explore include:

"What skills does an agent utilize on a daily basis?"
"How does this role differ from other roles in the organization?"
"What type of candidates are we looking to attract?"
"Is the position inbound or outbound?"
"Is the position full time or part time?"
"What hours will the agents be working?"
"What are some of the key skill sets required?"
"How much of a factor does technology play in the role?"
"How critical is the role to the effectiveness of the organization?"

4. The bond between management and agent is a bond made up of trust. The more confusion about pay, the less trust will be established

Employees feel entitled to show a lack of commitment when management flip-flops. They feel a loss of confidence in their superiors, all of which leads to higher turnover. Any compensation plan must be developed correctly the first time, and implemented with a long-term approach in mind. Certainly, management has that objective when they begin developing a compensation plan. However, the way they start and they way they finish are two separate realities. I know. I have created my share of good, and poor, compensation plans. Flipping plans endangers relationships. And because relationships are a strong fabric between supervisor and agent, flipping compensation plans is tantamount to inviting desertion. What works and is extremely exciting very often outweighs what is practical. In other words, management exclaiming "we need to get a compensation plan completed" oftentimes overrides their taking the time to write, plan and explore a truly successful compensation plan. A call center is somewhat like a large floating vessel. When there is confusion, more and more crew will disembark from the vessel and keep on walking. Consistent compensation agreements done correctly the first time between parties in the call center keep employees working on the ship. There is no reason why creating a compensation plan should cause agents to post warning flags. Take a glance back through the history of your call center and count the number of times compensation has changed. In one call center I managed, that count was twice in almost three years. Not bad, but still too much for me. It meant that in a three-year span there were three different plans. When we announced a plan change, most agents were not used to a switch, and they reacted cautiously. In another call center I managed, there were nine to eleven plan changes each year. Nine to eleven! What in the world were we thinking? In the process of each change, the relationship of trust took a severe beating. Agents knew, through past history, that the plan of today would not be the plan of tomorrow. Most plan changes were poorly designed, as well. That's why we kept changing the plans. In essence, we invited our agents to desert our ship every time we reached a new port.

> **Agents want to be paid steady and well. They recognize they can't "break the bank", because they recognize that corporations have budgets.**

I am a proponent of employee focus groups to facilitate the designing of compensation plans. This, of course, can open up a can of worms. The initial drawback is that agents will talk among one another about the plan. (Therefore, a proposal today becomes a concrete mistake tomorrow) However, the alternative to not asking for agent feedback is to develop a plan that falls short of doing what you need it to do. In a survey, various compensation questions may be asked. Asking the question "Would you like a higher base salary?" won't tell you anything. But asking "Will agents take less of a base salary to possibly earn more compensation in bonuses, commissions and incentives?" gives you a general idea of what agents might accept. Another question is "Is it important to you that management provide consistent prizes, awards and incentives to complement a compensation plan?" A third question can be "Would team bonuses and bonuses in addition to your salary based upon measured goals motivate you less than a simple compensation plan which relies on individual performance?" Meetings involve agents in some form of "buy-in". Management can always develop a compensation plan that works for them, but can they develop a truly spectacular compensation plan that works for them, their agents, and the entire company? That is the trick of encouraging "buy-in". When agents "buy-in", compensation agreements shine. I am a strong believer in also forming a "compensation team" to make certain that employees have a say in their compensation. A compensation team represents the ultimate "buy-in" because it forms the ultimate basis of trust. In forming a "compensation team", management could incorporate a mix of senior agents, middle agents and rookie agents, along with team leads and administrative personnel. Or, management could allow all agents to select a mixture of agents who form the compensation team for a period of one year. When changes are required, the team provides consultation and input. The process is a collaboration. Agents who live and die by the plan are far more likely to recognize what requirements need to be met to achieve the goals of the entire department, as well as the goals of the agents. And by being involved in the creation of a compensation agreement, those compensation team members lend an element of credibility to the plan.

5. A compensation agreement must be based on measured objectives with no discrepancy

No discrepancy. Too often, management pays their employees based on one objective, only to learn that another objective is more critical to the call center's success. Very often, management puts in place a compensation agreement without creating solid rules of operation to support the agreement. Agents are inundated with concerns and fears, because while the compensation plan appears solid, the loopholes are grand. If an agreement leaves open any doubt about measurement or objectives, the plan will falter. There should be no room for doubt. What is the goal? What will the goal be six months from now?

6. Pay agents based on what you want them to make, regardless of industry averages

Call center agents accept compensation plans based on conditioning from their environment and management. If an agent accepts a position for $7.50 per hour and a monthly team bonus, then the agent assumes this is the way compensation for that job works. I encourage management to create *their* standards for a position. The needs of one company may not work for another.

7. Don't be afraid to play with BIG NUMBERS or create unique standards

I have found that simple compensation agreements usually fail because they lack opportunity. Once a person becomes good at their job, the job becomes simple. A well-designed and creative compensation plan provides another boost to the job. For example, suppose one hundred full-time agents in your call center earn $9.00 per hour. What if you paid them $8.00 per hour? What if you took the savings ($800.00 per day, $4000.00 per week, $17,200 every month) and applied that savings to measurements that could reward every agent with far more than their basic $9.00 per hour?

To illustrate, suppose the most important objective in your call center is available time. At the moment 30% of your agents have available time between 75-100%. Budget the $17,200 you saved for 50% of agents to meet the goal of available time between 75-100%. If 50% of agents meet their goal next month, they each get a $344.00 bonus, which is $172.00 **_more_** than they would have received if they had their basic compensation plan of $9.00 per hour. If only 40% of agents meet the goal, then there is even more money to go around, ($430.00 per agent) or more money next month to spend. Management has now created a compensation plan that rewards call center agents for doing what they are required to do anyhow. This plan excites agents to meet objectives that must be met. Agents feel motivated when presented the opportunity to strive for something unique.

Creative Compensation

While money is the prime factor of compensation agreements, using creative compensation can go quite a long way in earning results and forging trust with your agents. I like to think of creative compensation as incentive that doesn't involve cash. I attended a call center conference once where the speaker talked about giving away seven or eight full-scale automobiles as part of a compensation plan. Certainly, not all businesses have the budget this company had, but most businesses don't realize that they are not far off from having the ability to do something spectacular with creative compensation.

For instance, if your staff is comprised of one hundred full-time employees earning $10.00 per hour and you change the compensation plan to pay them $8.50 per hour, your firm now has held on to over $1200.00 per day, which equates to $25,800.00 in the month. By simply dropping everyone's base salary by $1.50 per hour, each employee can be in a grand-prize drawing every month for a brand-new top-of-the-line automobile. Is reducing everyone's base salary by $1.50 per hour worth the motivation of awarding twelve of the one hundred agents brand new cars every year? Each business is different. (those twelve agents may think so!)

When it comes to outbound telesales compensation plans, I weight the commission plan extremely generously. In essence, the more sales or widgets one sells, the greater pay they can earn. The scale escalates. It is imperative that the first-rate agents, the superstars, earn the greatest money. They are your producers, and they need to be rewarded for producing. I weight the plan after the first 20% of sales has been completed. Therefore, instead of paying $50 a sale from sale number one through ten, I usually pay sale number one through ten at $10 per sale, and I take the money I saved and apply it for those who meet or exceed goal. I attempt to keep the base salary of outbound telesales agents lower than usual with a greater weight on commission because the job of outbound teleselling is a strenuous game. If the agent had a high base to fall back on, he / she wouldn't be as motivated to keep taking rejection one time after another. By keeping the commission plan high, the agent is forced to push forward and focus on making money, and, in particular, big money.

Summary

- New compensation agreements revolve around emotions, change and money. I implore management to recognize these three concepts as they go about changing a compensation agreement.

- Money drives performance, and performance is expected to drive money. Agents expect to receive quality compensation for quality work.

- Motivation, adulation, incentives and time-off all can be parts of a plan that make a compensation agreement succeed long-term.

- Management must be aware of how much money and investment the company is able to make in the call center.

- A compensation plan must be centered on the objectives of each particular job.

- Too often, companies change their compensation agreements continuously with little thought about consequences. This flip-flop of wages demonstrates to employees a severe disorganization among upper management and a lack of empathy by upper management for their employees' stability.

- If the objective of management when designing a call center compensation plan is to discourage turnover and increase the relationship between agent and manager, the plan must be developed correctly the first time, and implemented with a long-term approach in mind.

- If a compensation agreement is established that leaves open any doubt on measurement or objectives, the compensation plan will falter, both in implementation and in the eyes of agents.

- Call center agents accept compensation plans based on conditioning from their environment and management. If an agent accepts a position for $7.50 per hour with a monthly team bonus, then the agent assumes this is how compensation for that job works.

- Within the parameters of your call center, it is extremely important to conduct focus groups to involve agents in their opportunities.

- A well-designed and creative compensation plan provides another boost to the job. Therefore, don't be afraid to play with BIG NUMBERS or create unique standards.

CHAPTER 23

Performance Development Programs

"If an agent has poor performance periods, management must have a stable and well-outlined improvement plan to get them where they, and the customer contact center, need to be."   Dan Coen

Whether your call center is a sales operation or a customer service operation, it is mandatory that your staff is judged and motivated to an extent that drives them to perform above standards. Developing a serious and clear improvement program is extremely important to ensure that your staff gets the feedback, opportunities and penalties that they may deserve. Without a performance development program, your call center agents and supervisors are missing opportunities to increase performance and impact retention.

Perhaps you have heard the phrase that "everybody likes limits". A performance development plan sets the limits for agents. If an agent has poor performance periods, management must have a stable and well-outlined improvement plan to get them where they, and the customer contact center, need to be. If the agent can't perform to standards, management must have a solid policy of dismissal that they follow. A performance development program sets limits that management and agents follow so each party is on the same track. It eliminates the subjectivity.

In a majority of the call centers that I have visited, limits are benign, if nonexistent. Agents who have a sales goal aren't penalized when their goal isn't met. In addition, they aren't put on a development track to ensure their skill level will increase so the next month's goal will be met. And when put on a program, the program is generally weak and ineffective. There is no residual training and focus on problems when training and focused is desired. In essence, bottom feeders stay employed because management doesn't have a program in place to ensure they can terminate employees. Management also doesn't have a program in place to help bottom feeders grow. Your call center must have a performance development program to establish the motivation, incentive and focus that a bottom feeder performer wants.

Every job must present value. A performance development plan lays the limits and value for agents so their jobs become something more than a place merely to do work. In many cases, those who excel at their jobs desire a specific and critical performance development program for those who do not. I have been in many situations where top-level agents have asked me why our performance development plan was not more strict in order to weed out the poor performers. By making it more strict and by weeding out the poor performers, the performance development plan provides value to the high achievers, and validates their hard work and success.

A quality performance development plan should accomplish a few simple goals. First, it should provide management with an objective outlet to terminate employees. In the old days, firing an employee subjectively worked well. When it *seemed* as if the employee wasn't capable of performing, it was time to terminate him. Today, the *feel* part of supervision must go away. There must be solid goals, enforced and measured, in order to terminate employees. A performance development program does just that. Second, a performance development program allows management and agents to partner to improve performance when improved performance is warranted. The program should be about far more than simply terminating employees. It should involve elements of coaching, one-on-one communication, residual training, and increased attention. Management should have a written and focused plan to improve the performance of those agents in a call center who are on the performance development program. A performance development program is a structured program for supervisors and agents to ensure that everything that can be done is being done to improve performance levels. Third, a quality performance development program sets the limits that ensures most agents will do everything they can to stay off the program. In the customer contact center, the motivation to stay off the plan serves as an enticement to do well. Whereas agents may not have performed well in the month of March because there was no reason to, the very introduction of the performance development program provides those same agents with a reason to improve performance. They usually do.

To develop a performance development program for your telesales or customer service operation, use the following points as a foundation.

1. A Performance Development Program Must Be Enforced.
2. A Performance Development Program Must Be Practical And Simple.
3. A Performance Development Program Must Be Fair.
4. A Performance Development Program Must Include Training.
5. A Performance Development Program Must Grandfather In Existing Agents.
6. A Performance Development Program Must Be Executed Based On Specific And Relevant Objectives.

7. A Performance Development Program Must Provide Management With Flexibility.

Here are questions supervisors should ask of themselves to do just that:

1. What Do You Want Your Call Center To Look Like?

2. How Do You Want To Manage Your Call Center?

3. How Do You Want Your Agents To View Your Call Center?

4. Can You Impact The Call Center Consistently?

5. Today, Does Your Call Center Appeal To A Broad Range of Agents?

6. What Is The Proven Track Record Of Your Call Center?

7. How Does Your Competition Reach Out To Their Agents?

8. What Type Of Environment Does Your Call Center Communicate?

9. Is Your Call Center Adaptable And Changeable?

10. What steps do you have in place to encourage agent feedback?

Each of the above questions is designed to provide the supervisor with the ability of introspection. If a supervisor has little interest in the questions or in providing answers, the supervisor is demonstrating little passion for the task at hand. For instance, notice question number eight: "What type of environment does your call center communicate?" This requires introspection to formulate the answer.

Most call centers sparkle when a telesales performance development plan has strong standards to eliminate the "focal point", or middle agents, quickly. I am a firm proponent of having supervisors work incredibly hard with new agents to get them ramped up quickly. Those agents who fail to meet minimum goals over an extended period, but become part of the "wall- paper" of the company, are the agents that lower performance results. New agents need to be worked with. Superstar agents need to be rewarded for exceeding performance goals. Focal point agents, those in the middle, must perform or leave. Performance programs are designed to continually raise the bar, increase the goals, and have a call center with very little middle class.

Below are some general techniques when creating performance development programs:

1. The program must have clearly outlined objectives

If agents are expected to meet goals or be placed on a program, then the objectives must be defined so there is no confusion. Sounds easy, but it never is. Factors such as days, weeks, months and quarters come into play. A new program for new agents must be created to ensure they have clearly outlined objectives.

2. The program must have a development piece

Although agents get penalized by going on a performance development program when they fail to meet goals, the program should be flexible enough to train agents to improve their performance so they can eventually get off the program.

3. The program must be implemented, not ignored, by supervisors

It's easy to fail to put some agents on the program when they don't meet goals, but what does that say to those agents who are on the program, or who think they may be put on the program in the future. The most difficult thing for a supervisor to do is to enforce the program and terminate an employee. Once that is done, however, the message is sent.

4. Consistency is important. The program can't continually be changed

Agents want a level of comfort. They want to believe that management knows what they are doing. They don't want to be part of a program that management can't get correct. A well thought out program must be supported for six months to a year to see how valuable the program is.

5. The program must not have too many, or too few, participants

Ten or twenty percent of your group should be on the program at any one time. If more are on the program, then various questions need to be asked. Is the program overly strict? Are the goals out of place? is training merely adequate and not world class? If so, how can it be improved? Is hiring inadequate?

CHAPTER 24

Delivering Monitoring Checklists

"The value in a checklist exists for the agent, not the manager."
Dan Coen

I have always enjoyed delivering monitoring checklists to agents. Obviously, it forced me as the manager to spend one-on-one time with the agents, and that extremely valuable form of communication cannot be overrated. There were many times when I didn't want to spend what I considered to be <u>my valuable time</u> sitting down with an agent to talk about their telephone skills. However, it so happens that each time I performed a monitoring checklist and sat down with a particular employee, <u>my valuable time</u> became much less important to me, and much more of a value to that agent.

As a manager, so much of your work is divided in so many different directions that the monitoring checklist is forgotten. Yet, in the call center, the monitoring checklist is the most valued, but least performed, task. The majority of your telephone agents truly relish monitoring checklists, even if they will not admit so. They want feedback on what they do well, and they need feedback on what they can be doing better to find more success. Certainly, there are a few telephone agents who will wish they never had the manager pull up a chair and deliver a monitoring checklist, but that is natural in any field of business, and those agents have valid reasons for feeling that way. But by and large, agents cry out for monitoring checklists. They are the "touch-and-feel" of the relationship between manager and agent.

Senior executives find it very difficult to get management to perform monitoring checklists. The value in a checklist exists for the agent, not the manager. At first glance, the manager perceives very little reason to take the time to do a monitoring checklist. Therefore, it is the job of senior management to paint clearly and precisely why management must regularly do monitoring checklists. Some reasons are as follows:

♦ They force the manager to spend one-on-one time with the agents.
♦ They demonstrate to the agents that management wants to help improve their performance.

♦ Monitoring Checklists can be used to track performance standards over an extended period, and should be filed to help administer with performance reviews.

♦ They allow agents to provide feedback about anything on their minds that they otherwise might not willingly come forward to address.

♦ Monitoring Checklists allow management to gauge areas of improvement.

♦ Monitoring Checklists allow management to recognize superior performance.

♦ Monitoring Checklists allow management to residually train agents in a focused setting.

♦ Monitoring Checklists assist third parties, such as the client or executive personnel, to observe the performance of agents.

Monitoring checklists are a form of supervisor / agent communication that is unique to the call center world. Few other departments have a system where management listens to an employee, subjectively critiques that employee's work, and then spends from five minutes to one hour training the employee with regard to what the manager heard, and how the employee may improve to add to success for everybody.

Every client and project is different, but I believe monitoring checklists should be performed no less than once each month, per employee. Every project is different, but many projects require as much as one monitoring checklist a day or one monitoring checklist a week, etc, based on such factors as management-to-agent ratios, number of work hours in the week, length of checklists, length of counseling sessions, etc. To get a true flavor of how an agent performs, once every month is the least amount of time a manager should spend monitoring and then presenting a monitoring checklist to the agent.

There are many ways to perform monitoring checklists. Let's explore each one and discuss their benefits and drawbacks.

♦ Listen to tapes of calls

I am not a big believer in listening to taped calls, because I am a big proponent of instant training. If a manager monitors from a tape, the manager misses a golden opportunity to counsel the agent as training is warranted. In addition, when the supervisor sits with the agent and begins counseling him, the impact of his calls is lessened. When performing checklists from a tape, the agent is always defending himself, saying such lines as "I did it then but I don't do that now," and "I just don't remember that call". Any time factor from monitoring a call to counseling the call dissipates the impact of training. I am a big proponent, however, of taping calls so agents may hear their actual calls on-line. One of the premier ways to better provide agents with residual training is to allow them the chance to hear themselves talking. How many times have I seen agents light up when listening to themselves? How many times have agents exclaimed "I didn't know I sounded like that!" How many times have I used tapes to make points about how to better communicate on the telephone? The answers are infinite. Another positive of taped calls is that listening to taped calls allows the supervisor to hear calls after the day is over, giving him plenty of time to develop his monitoring checklist. The supervisor can listen to each call more than once and spend time developing his thoughts about what should be done and could be done to make call performance better. One of the drawbacks of listening to a call live is that the supervisor has very little time to digest and train before hearing another call. By using the tape, the supervisor can think about what areas he needs to address with the agent.

◆ Monitor the agent from the manager's office so the agent doesn't recognize that management is monitoring

The lazy-man supervisor will sit in his office and monitor his agents via the telephone. When I manage supervisors, I dislike seeing them stuck in their office, because their primary effectiveness, as we have explored in other chapters, is on the call center floor. Therefore, a supervisor monitoring in his office loses much of the personal interaction that means most to the agent. However, one cannot overvalue the importance of listening to agent calls without the agent knowing. When you "plug in" next to the agent, you will get from your employee exactly what you want. The agent will manipulate his presentation to ensure that the shortcuts, slips and easy paths he may utilize when you are not listening disappear when you are listening. Once you leave, he goes right back to what he enjoys doing most, even if that isn't best for himself or the company.

◆ Monitor the agent while sitting side-by-side with the agent

This is the best way to monitor an agent. It forces agent and supervisor to have quality communication and relations, and it ties the supervisor and agent into a special triangle: Supervisor, Agent, Prospect. The large drawback to monitoring side-by-side is that the agent will do exactly what the supervisor wants the agent to do. While monitoring in an office or through listening to a tape, the supervisor obtains a more honest presentation. When the supervisor sits next to the agent, the agent shapes up. Yet, the value of having the supervisor coach the agent during the call cannot be overestimated. Using the notepad, or a mute button, the supervisor can provide advice to the agent. And, the value of instant feedback immediately after a call is completed cannot be discounted.

How to present a review

♦ **Develop a theme around the review**

What do you want accomplished when you sit next to the agent? Is the review positive, middle of the road, or a true training session to improve sales skills. Always attempt to provide a theme of the review so the agent understands the exact purpose of the meeting. For instance, if the agent will only glean a certain number of points from a twenty minute monitoring review session, make the first point you deliver the most valuable: the theme. A theme may be "I was very impressed with what I heard, and I have a few pointers that will make you even that much more successful."

♦ **Be succinct with regard to each of the objectives on the review form. Provide examples.**

When delivering a review, put yourself in your agent's shoes. What does he need to hear in order to gain training from this session? I have been caught presenting what I wanted to present to the agent without realizing that I was talking on tangents and moving the conversation all over the place. The agent wasn't learning. Using a monitoring form as guidance, go right down the form and be specific on each point. It is okay to look at a point and say "this was fine, I have nothing to say." However, make sure you point that out.

♦ **Don't limit the review to just the objectives outlined on the form**

Inexperienced supervisors go over the form and provide the agent with a copy. This meets their objective. However, supervisors who are doing the review to benefit the agent will use every category, the side margins, the back of the page, etc. The supervisor will provide agents with handouts from the internet or magazine articles to benefit their learning.

♦ **Ask agents for critiques of themselves**

This philosophy is similar to what I teach in telesales training workshops. As a presenter, it is silly to focus on your thoughts, ideas and desires when the other person has those similar thoughts, ideas and desires. Ask them what they are thinking. Their thinking will help you present to them how you can help. Perhaps the agent may say "I just feel like I can't close", or "I feel good about my presentation, but I can't get through the opening."

◆ Provide examples when asking for improvement

How many times have you told somebody how to do something without showing them how to make it happen? During monitoring reviews, use role plays and examples to give them the learning tools they need. This can be done for product knowledge issues, as well as telesales and communications training, and computer training involving e-mail or web analysis.

◆ Consider doing role-playing or listening to tapes

I am a big believer in listening to tapes. Many times, agents say "Holy cow, I didn't know I sounded like that." By listening to themselves, an agent learns what they did right or wrong on calls. This is invaluable.

◆ Go over the objectives for the next review carefully

Build each review for the next review. Use each learning critique as a follow-up for the next technique. Monitoring checklists work when they form a ladder to the next step. For instance, perhaps a program can be developed which takes into account three monitoring checklists. Each checklist builds to the next checklist, and the performance improvement programs put into place are followed closely by supervisor and agent. Every monitoring review performed must have a plan for the next review.

ABOUT US

Dan Coen has dedicated his career to call center operations, direct marketing, management, and sales. He is an authority on building call centers, managing direct marketing and sales campaigns, motivating agents, integrating technology and e-commerce within the customer contact center, and customizing training workshops and strategies for professionals nationwide. Dan's first book and workbook **Friendly Persuasion: Dynamic Telephone Sales Training and Techniques for the 21st Century,** *studies telesales training and communication for any professional that sells and communicates via the telephone. He lives in Los Angeles.*

Dan Coen
DCD Publishing
PO Box 571533
Tarzana, CA 91357
888-835-5326 (book orders)
818-703-1022 (telephone and fax)
dcddcd@aol.com
www.dcdpublishing.com

Order These Books And Workbooks
From DCD Publishing

888-835-5326

Building Call Center Culture   WORKBOOK
*Strategies for designing a world class performance-based
environment within your customer contact center*

Friendly Persuasion   BOOK
*Dynamic Telephone Sales Training And Techniques For The
21st Century*

Friendly Persuasion   WORKBOOK
*Dynamic Telephone Sales Training And Techniques For The
21st Century*

65 Techniques To Manage Call Center Agents   BOOK
*Extraordinary tactics and effective philosophies to enhance su-
pervision of your customer contact representatives
(COMING JUNE, 2001)*

Powerful Workshops And Tailored Consulting Strategies For Your Business

DCD Publishing provides a customized and unprecedented full service partnership for those who desire experienced, hands-on consulting, seminars, training books, workbooks and special projects.

Contact Dan Coen

Dan Coen
DCD Publishing
PO Box 571533
Tarzana, CA 91357
888-835-5326   (book orders)
818-703-1022   (telephone and fax)
dcddcd@aol.com
www.dcdpublishing.com

VicePresidents.com

Center For The Study Of The Vice Presidency

www.vicepresidents.com

Featured Sites	*Interactions*
Stories and Snapshots	*Biographies*
Fun Facts	*Also Nominees*
Historical Analysis	*Vice Presidential Trivia*
Books	*Links*
Commentaries and Features	*Research Papers*

"We study the Vice Presidency like no other internet magazine."

www.vicepresidents.com